AILING CITIES

HISTORY ASSESSMENT AND REMEDY FOR URBANIZATION IN GHANA

Kwaku L. Keddey

Published by Applied Research and Design Publishing,
an imprint of ORO Editions.
Gordon Goff: Publisher

www.appliedresearchanddesign.com
info@appliedresearchanddesign.com

Copyright © 2021 Kwaku L. Keddey.

All rights reserved. No part of this book may be reproduced, stored in a retrieval system, or transmitted in any form or by any means including electronic, mechanical, photocopying of microfilming, recording, or otherwise (except that copying permitted by Sections 107 and 108 of the U.S. Copyright Law and except by reviewers for the public press) without written permission from the publisher.

You must not circulate this book in any other binding or cover and you must impose this same condition on any acquirer.

Author: Kwaku L. Keddey

Book Design: Ahankara Art

Project Manager: Jake Anderson

10 9 8 7 6 5 4 3 2 1 First Edition

ISBN: 978-1-954081-08-6

Color Separations and Printing: ORO Group Ltd.

Printed in China.

AR+D Publishing makes a continuous effort to minimize the overall carbon footprint of its publications. As part of this goal, AR+D, in association with Global ReLeaf, arranges to plant trees to replace those used in the manufacturing of the paper produced for its books. Global ReLeaf is an international campaign run by American Forests, one of the world's oldest nonprofit conservation organizations. Global ReLeaf is American Forests' education and action program that helps individuals, organizations, agencies, and corporations improve the local and global environment by planting and caring for trees.

AILING CITIES

HISTORY ASSESSMENT AND REMEDY FOR URBANIZATION IN GHANA

APPLIED RESEARCH +DESIGN PUBLISHING

NOVATO, CA

CONTENTS

INTRODUCTION 6

REVIVE ACCRA OR BUILD A NEW CAPITAL CITY? 13

  The Rise of Accra: Pre-Independence... 13
  Urban Planning in Accra 14
  Ills of Modern Accra 16
  Calls for a New Capital 63 Years After Independence 21
  Future of Accra 25
  Founding a City 28

CHANGE IN A CLIMATE CHANGE ERA 31

  Perennial Flooding in Ghana 31
  Understanding Climate Change 35
  Adapting to Climate Change 41
  Urban Heat Island Effect (UHI).. 44
  Sustainable and Resilient Infrastructure 47
  How do we Achieve the Sustainability and Resilience Agenda? .. 48
  Taking Advantage of the Sun 52
  Making Coastal Cities Resilient: Elmina 54

PARKS AND URBAN FORESTRY 57

  Saving the Vegetative Cover of an Urbanizing Accra 60
  Protecting the Vegetation Zones... 63
  Avoiding Extinction 65

A RELOOK AT THE TRANSPORTATION MODES 67

  The Revival of Rail Transport 70
  Toward a Vibrant Ghanaian Railway Sector 74
  Revolutionizing Cycling 76

ACCESSIBLE AND AFFORDABLE HOUSING 80

  Housing in Ghana 83
  Ghana Housing Policy... 86
  The Ghanaian's Right to Housing 89
  How Have Other Countries Approached Housing? 90
  The Suburbanization Culture Explained....................................... 91

Making Persons with Disability (PWD) Special..........................95
Housing Prisoners and Making Prisons Model Communities ...97

SLUMS AND SQUATTER SETTLEMENT 100

The Issue of Population Explosion 100
Defining Slums 103
The Global Picture 105
Life of the Slum Dweller 106
Growth of Slums 107
Old Fadama: Slum Upgrading or Slum Clearance?....................108
Learning from Curitiba 112

ZONING AND MASTER PLANNING.. 114

Plan Making and Zoning in Principle 116
Zoning in Ghana 120
Land Ownership in Ghana 121
Ethical Land Use 123
Mortgage Financing 124
Protecting the City's Image 126
Planning Terminologies..127

STREET LAYOUT AND CITY PLANNING.. 130

Grid Street System 131
Radial Street System 134
The Industrial Revolution 135
Urban Renewal 136

RECOMMENDATIONS FOR THE FUTURE OF GHANAIAN CITIES... 137

Economic Development 138
Community Engagement 138
Parks and Tree Planting 139
Alternative Modes of Transport 140
Future of Ghanaian Prisons 141
Built Environment Institutions and the Thriving City 141
Role of Young Planners..143

NOTES 146
BIBLIOGRAPHY 156

INTRODUCTION

At the turn of the fifteenth century when European powers acquired geographical knowledge and advanced navigation skills, the African continent became an important destination. Their initial interest was in spices like nutmeg, cloves, pepper, and cinnamon, but Africa had none to offer. In the Gold Coast (present-day Ghana) it was no different, but they found something more valuable—gold and slaves. Ghana is a country blessed with many natural resources. These resources have been exploited since 1471 when Portuguese sailors landed on its shores and found gold within a few miles of the sea.[2] They later discovered gold producing areas around the Ankobra and Volta rivers. Ghana became known as the "Gold Coast" because of these discoveries.[3] By the sixteenth century, Ghana's supply of gold was so significant that it attracted other European powers, notably the Danish, Dutch, Swedish, French, German, and British. This is evidenced by the numerous ports and castles built during their trips.[4] By 1642, the Dutch had ousted the Portuguese from Ghana. Besides the slave trade, the Europeans played a key role in the spread of many South American plants in Africa. These plants included maize (of Mexican origin), cassava, haricot beans, ground nut, tomato, pawpaw, naseberry, pineapple, red pepper, and cocoa, and spread throughout the tropical world, and from which Ghana substantially benefitted.[5]

There was a concentration of slave traders in the Gold Coast. The slave trade thrived particularly because the people of the Gold Coast found value in cloth, hardware, metals, firearms, and so on, in exchange for gold and slaves. Slaves were mostly bought from kings, chiefs, and merchants and the sheer volume of trade led the Europeans to lease land from the local people to build forts that were architectural monuments then and now:[6] in Accra, Ada, Apam, Anomabu, Anashan, Akwida, Beraku, Beyin, Butri, Cape Coast, Dixcove, Elmina, Egya, Keta, Kormantine, Komenda, Mori, Mingo, Osu, Prampram, Shama, Sekondi, Takoradi, Takrama, Tesh, Tantamkweri, and Winneba.[7] The slaves provided the solution to the humanpower needs of the agricultural enterprises in the American tropics. European labor was expensive and these laborers were not as willing to comply with the demands of the work as was the case with African slaves.[8]

At the beginning of the nineteenth century the British, Dutch and Danish were the only European nations that actively participated in trade on the Gold Coast.[9] The slave trade was vibrant on the coast for many years, but when profits started to dwindle, the Dutch and the Danish were reluctant to remain in the Gold Coast. They sold their forts to the British and departed. The Danish handed over their forts (Christiansborg, Keta, Ada, Ningo, and Teshi) in 1850 and the Dutch handed over their fort in 1872 (Elmina, Komenda, Shama, Sekondi, Butri, Dixcove, Axim, and Beyin). This laid the path for the British to assert their authority over the entire Gold Coast. In 1874 the Gold Coast became a British Colony.[10] There were other European nations operating in several countries in Africa, but as demand for raw materials became very acute and competitive, the quest to control the source of supply of raw materials (cotton, rubber, and minerals) to Europe from Africa during the Industrial Revolution became intense. This resulted in a race to invest surplus capital and find markets for overproduction of goods, ultimately leading to the scramble for the African continent by France, Germany, Italy, England, Portugal, and Belgium.[11] In the scramble for Africa, statespersons and diplomats met in offices and country houses in Europe and drew lines across maps with no regard to culture, ethnicity, and other characteristics that defined the people and shaped their way of life. The frontiers had to be traced along lines of latitude and longitude because of the lack of geographical detail.[12] This led to the frontiers of the Gold Coast becoming devoid

Christianborg Castle, Accra

of natural unity by population distribution or physical geography; the seed had been sown for future problems. People from the same tribe ended up being separated by frontiers; the Ewes, Mossis, and Dagombas were split between Ghana, Ivory Coast, and Togo respectively.[13] Despite the issues surrounding the frontiers, Ghana's wealth was unmatched. It was the third largest producer of rubber in the world at the close of the nineteenth century (1890). Ghana exported gold, rubber, palm oil, and ivory for decades. When Tetteh Quarshie started planting cocoa seeds he had received from a brother in Fernando Po in 1879, little did he know he was adding to the wealth of Ghana. Today, Ghana is the second largest producer of cocoa worldwide. However, the country's wealth did not trickle down to the majority of people. In 1899 the Ashanti Goldfields had commenced operations in Ghana, but a pittance was paid for the concessions obtained by the mining companies from the local rulers, and they persistently refused to pay any royalties on profits. This was voiced by Nana Sir Ofori Atta I in 1939 in the Legislative Assembly of Ghana.[14] A reconnaissance survey undertaken by the Department of Geological Survey in 1945 discovered deposits of manganese at Nsuta, diamond at Birim Valley, bauxite at Nyinahin, Sefwi Bekwai, Mpraeso, Kibi, and iron ore near Shiene.[15]

The paltry benefits accrued from exploration of precious minerals in the Gold Coast was attributed to colonial rule by the local people, and after independence in 1957 there was a lot of pomp and pageantry in expectation of economic prosperity as a result of this exploration of natural resources. This belief was also ignited by the coming into office of the first president, Osagyefo Dr. Kwame Nkrumah, a man the historian W.E.F. Ward described as "having the personal charm, captivating eloquence, and gifts of leadership that made men follow him." President Nkrumah started the running of the country with hope but his stay in power was short-lived because of a coup d'état in 1966. The overthrow of governments became a common occurrence between 1966 and 1981. Political instability was the norm until 1992 when the country returned to constitutional rule and democracy was solidified.

In 2008 oil was discovered in commercial quantities in Ghana and with it renewed hope that, finally, the oil revenue would bring the needed change to the economy and usher in a new dawn of prosperity and development, especially in the western region. However, 12 years after the discovery and production of oil, there is little to show for it.

Ghanaians fought courageously for their independence, but 63 years later economic freedom still remains more of a dream than reality. Corruption, indiscipline, nepotism, lack of political will, and lack of commitment seem to have infiltrated every facet of the society. The country is still economically dependent on the same foreign powers many blamed for destroying a nation with so many prospects. It feels as if Ghana is still experiencing a new form of indirect rule. During colonial rule, even though each colony under the British had its own governance, the policy of indirect rule through native institutions was adopted for all. Chieftaincy, customary law, and practice were allowed to flourish. Ghana was under the leadership of a governor, who reported to a secretary of state for colonies. The governor was assisted by a partly nominated legislative council and an executive council.[16] One would ask, have traditional leaders failed Ghanaians? They had the power to prevent a lot of the issues that confront Ghana today, but disputes associated with land acquisition and ownership, mineral concessions, impact on community development, as well as forest degradation persist.

Surprisingly, with all the activities of the Europeans in the country over centuries, Ghanaian cities do not depict any vitality. They have grown with less guidance and law enforcement by local authorities, hence the perennial problems of floods during the raining seasons, outbreak of epidemics, among other issues. Article 257 (6) of the 1992 Constitution of Ghana provides that "Every mineral in its natural state in, under or upon any land in Ghana, rivers, streams, water course throughout Ghana, the exclusive economic zone and any area covered by the territorial sea or continental shelf is the property of the Republic of Ghana and shall be vested in the president on behalf of, and in trust for the people of Ghana." A percentage of revenue received from the sale of such resources must be consciously and continuously used to develop cities with infrastructure services such as water, sanitation, parks, roads, etc. Many citizens have questioned if the political leaders of Ghana are cognizant of the deterioration of cities, and how the future generation will be impacted if sustainable solutions are not found to the many problems.

The year 2020 will forever be remembered as the year of the coronavirus, which caught the world by surprise. Economies worldwide both large and small have been ravaged by the pandemic, and the impact remains incalculable. The situation in sub-Saharan

Africa is scarier because of the poverty that is associated with majority of its countries. After three weeks of partial lockdown, the economy of Ghana was in distress according to Finance Minister Ken Ofori Atta in his article from April 16, 2020 in the *Financial Times* newspaper titled "What Does an African Finance Minister do Now?" He had to adopt a different strategy to make up for the loss in revenue as domestic taxes continued to decline and the losses were further compounded by the diminution in employment figures. The partial lockdown proved ineffective because of the nature of settlements in our cities. Such an experience presents an opportunity for a careful assessment of Ghanaian cities, especially those with large populations like Accra, Kumasi, Tamale, and Takoradi. This is a wakeup call for the citizenry to demand better policies and goals from both the central government and traditional rulers. Learning from cities around the world and how they have tackled similar issues is necessary. Building developments in many of the cities in Ghana are not high rise, and as such, putting in remedial measures at this stage may be prudent.[18] Most importantly, present and future governments must work with experts (architects, engineers, and planners) to lead the transformation of our cities to achieve the "Ghana Beyond Aid" agenda.

CHAPTER 1
REVIVE ACCRA OR BUILD A NEW CAPITAL CITY?

The Rise of Accra: Pre-Independence

Accra was founded in the latter part of the sixteenth century by the Ga people.[1] It was a small fishing town; its name is the anglicized version of the Akan word *Nkran*, which means ants. Ga is the native name for Accra. The wealth and power wielded by Accra saw rapid growth, and by 1600 it was the most viable choice as the capital of the Ga Federation.[2] The Ga people grew more powerful in the early seventeenth century by establishing firm control over trade between the interior and the coast. The Ga kingdom was governed by a king and fetish priests. Ayawaso (13 kilometers from the coast) was the first site selected as the capital of the kingdom before being moved to the coast to enhance trade with the Portuguese. The growth and development of Accra could be attributed to the construction of three European forts as trading posts: the Ussher Fort (built by the Dutch in 1650), Christianborg Castle (built by the Swedes in 1657), and James Fort (built by the British in 1673).[3]

In 1877, a few years after the British had assumed political control of Ghana, they moved the capital from Cape Coast to Accra. Accra was preferred because of its climatic conditions, and the conduciveness of the population to taxation.[4] Climatic conditions were essential because of the drier climate in Accra compared with Cape Coast.[5] Accra is the only coastal savannah zone in Africa. Health related reasons were also key to the selection of Accra as the site for the colonial administration. Malaria, caused by the presence of mosquitoes, troubled the British settlers and prevented most of the Europeans from settling in Ghana permanently.[6] For centuries malaria has been the most widespread of tropical diseases and the most dangerous species of the Anopheles' carriers called Anopheles gambiae, which was dominant in Ghana. Malaria weakens people as bouts of fever continually sap physical strength and make them unfit for any meaningful work or endeavour.[7] Protection from other local diseases, through new development, was a prudent measure for the British colonial residents. The selection of Accra was not based on consensus and it is without doubt that Ghanaians did not play any substantial role in the decision to make Cape Coast the first capital city.[8]

Accra became the economic center of Ghana after the completion of the railway lines to the mining and agricultural areas located in the interior of the country.[9] The population of Accra rose from 17,892 in 1901 to 135,926 in 1948.[10] On the eve of independence in 1957, the population of Accra was 190,000. In 1960, the population was 338,000. The 1994 census recorded the city's population as 970,000.[11] By the turn of the century in 2000 the population was 1,658,937. The present population is estimated at 2.1 million, but others estimate it at 4 million.[12] Whatever the true number, the population is increasing exponentially and adequate measures have to be put in place to ensure that the infrastructure of the city can conveniently cater to the needs of the present and future occupants of the city. If urban planning is ignored, and institutions of the built environment are not adequately resourced and engaged to proffer sustainable solutions, then disaster surely awaits the city. There are enough examples in the history of the modern world to show that a city without a clear vision and a set of goals outlined by a comprehensive plan will eventually self-destruct. A plan is an adopted statement of policy, in the form of text, maps, and graphics, used to guide public and private actions that affect the future of a city.[13]

Urban Planning in Accra

Town councils were responsible for town planning and building control in the Gold Coast. After large portions of Accra were destroyed as a result of the earthquake of 1862, the colonial government saw it as an opportunity to rebuild and reorganize the city.[14] This was, however, not thoroughly done because Accra was not under the full control of any European nations. Even when the British took over control of Accra, urban planning was limited to state-controlled lands that accounted for only 13% of residential land in Accra (Ridge, Cantonments, Labone, etc.). The urban centers were divided into British and Ghanaian zones. Zoning and building codes were enforced to maintain an orderly character and ambiance in the British zones. The British zones were therefore characterized by buildings with lawns, flower gardens along paved streets with streetlights. The Ghanaian zones, on the other hand, were unplanned, squalid, overcrowded, and made up of houses without any artistic touch:[15] an example of such being the Nima and Maamobi residential areas that are adjacent to the Airport and Roman Ridge residential areas.[16] Customary lands were also neglected (Nima, Sabon Zongo, James Town). This led to crowded, cluttered, congested environment with poor structures and unhealthy conditions[17] in most parts of the city. Sir Frederick Gordon Guggisberg's 25-year development plan ensured that between 1919 and 1927 several development projects, such as schools and hospitals, were built but it did little to change the Ghanaian zones.[18]

In 1944 the first physical plan of Accra was prepared by Maxwell Fry to ensure the provision of sanitation, lighting, water, a market, a slaughterhouse, and streets. In 1958 another plan was drafted with the full elements of a masterplan by Alan Ford and B.D.W. Treavallion, but little implementation was carried out. The notable activity undertaken was the Ring Road industrial area.[19] Prime Minister Kwame Nkrumah had a different vision for the city upon taking power, which was not in line with the two earlier plans. Despite his best intentions, his stay in power was short-lived and his plans were not implemented to their fullest. Physical development planning has not been a success in Ghana. The short-term nature of development plans, unsuitable support structure to ensure the viability of the plans, mismanagement, and the numerous coup d'état by the military are some of the reasons for the failure of development planning in Ghana. Even though the last coup d'état was in 1981 when Dr. Hilla Limann was overthrown, the military government that was in power from 1981 to 1992 still missed the opportunity to undertake long term planning. In the 1980s, for instance, all undeveloped land within the city was under threat. Ineffective governmental control led to buildings springing up on open spaces and road reservations. People built without a title to land or planning permits. Wealth and political connections were all that was required to undertake illegal development. Even drainage ways and flood-prone areas in Dzorwulu, Airport West Residential Area, and Alajo were not spared.[20] The result is a congested city without parks and open areas. The sprawling of the city has also led to road infrastructure and water supply challenges.

The fact that not all metropolitan, municipal, and district assemblies (MMDAs) have their spatial development framework, structure plans, and local plans in place, coupled with the practice of chiefs (who are trustees of majority of customary lands) engaging the services of surveyors to prepare layouts for the purpose of sale, leads to development without the needed facilities accompanying it. Development thus occurs before structure plans are outlined to guide them.[21] The hiatus (1986–2005) that occurred in the training of spatial planners at the Kwame Nkrumah University of Science and Technology has also resulted in shortage of physical planning officers who must play a leading role in MMDAs. Staffing policy for the MMDAs for planning purposes is, therefore, a challenge. Generally, built environment professionals who have to see to the development of plans, inspection of buildings, and detection of illegal development are in short supply, and monitoring of these areas is low. Equally worrying is when some of the few planning officers that are available engage in alleged corrupt practices with developers by allowing development to take place without all the required permits. It is a known fact that until most built environment professionals sit for their professional examination, they have little to no prior knowledge of the building regulations and planning laws. Also, apprentice draughtmen undertake work of certified professionals in some instances at MMDAs.[22]

The results of what poor planning had done to Ghanaian cities became evident early in the 21st century. The only exception is the semblance of order in communities like the Airport Residential, Cantonments, North Labone, and Airport West that have roots in the influence of the British and the elite of Ghanaians who took over political control after independence. Generally, the city can best be described, from a planning perspective, as having no form and being spatially chaotic. Planners are yet to become active players in urban politics of Accra due to the persecution associated with the politics of Ghana. Most experienced planners prefer to be neutral observers and the Ghana Institute of Planners lack the required power to influence government decisions.[23]

Ills of Modern Accra

Accra has become overburdened with urban ills that threaten its future. The avid interest of Ghanaians in the growth of Accra has left many planning professionals with endless questions about the city's

Banana Inn, Accra

effectiveness as the administrative capital of Ghana. If taxation and a geographical concern were the main reasons for the change of the capital from Cape Coast to Accra, then presently, there are countless compelling reasons and conditions that support the urgent need to relocate Ghana's capital for the second time. In any case, the British concentrated their activities on the coastal regions to the neglect of the middle and northern sectors. What was the involvement of the native people in this decision to pick a new capital? What kind of stakeholder consultations were done? An evaluation of what is ideal for the Ghanaian and not what benefited the British should be the criteria for assessing Accra's effectiveness as a capital.

Accra covers a surface area of 173 km^2 and the Greater Accra Metropolitan Area (GAMA) covers 894 km^2. With an annual growth rate of 4.3%, the area has become overburdened with urban ills.[24] An illusion of economic opportunities has lured many people from all over Ghana into Accra. This movement has led to population increase coupled with a scramble for the limited and inadequate services available.[25] Even before independence, rural-urban migration was a factor in the growth of population. People came from different parts of the Gold Coast into the urban centers of Accra. Not all the migrants, made up of literate and illiterates from different tribal and cultural groups, succeeded in finding jobs. Without jobs, most migrants depended on employed family members for their survival instead of returning to rural life.[26] As more and more people migrated, the need for accommodation became a problem. They settled in non-European zones and others found new settlements that set sprawling (horizontal growth) in motion. Over the years, the sprawling of the city has hindered the provision of essential services (water, solid waste disposal, refuse collection, good drainage, and electricity). Provision of essential services to sprawling areas has become costly and difficult.[27] The existing facilities are also deteriorating due to lack of maintenance, and the needed injection of investment to overhaul these systems is not forthcoming.[28]

Presently, choked drains, indiscriminate waste disposal, open defecation, uncollected refuse in central waste containers—to name but a few—characterize the sanitation situation in Accra. The uncollected waste finds its way into water bodies and drainage systems and pose health risks to dwellers.[29] The burden on the drainage networks and the reliance on Pan/Bucket System and other unsanitary systems may cause serious problems if they are not mitigated.[30] Surprisingly, policy decisions on the sanitation situation in Accra have been debated since the 19th century. Overcrowding and poor sanitary conditions were prevalent in urban living environments of the Gold Coast, especially Accra. Policies and legislation were developed and implemented to curtail spread of diseases. For instance, hundreds of lives were lost as a result of the bubonic plague of 1907 in Accra.[31] The sanitation situation has not seen remarkable improvement despite the commendable efforts of private waste management companies like Zoomlion. The generation of waste is estimated at 1,800 tonnes with a capacity for collection at 1,200 tonnes per day. The monopoly of Zoomlion has its downsides, but until it is addressed, citizens can help make their work easier by adopting safe and sustainable waste management practices in urban communities.

Research has shown that the more sprawling experienced by a city leads to a high percentage of the family budget going into transportation. The increase in automobile use has made the vehicular traffic situation in Accra unbearable. The traffic congestion is constantly heavy as 65% of vehicular movement is to and from the central business district. The dominance of low-capacity vehicles and the high travel time makes the traffic an unpleasant experience daily.[32] Mass transit and railway have not been effective. Pedestrians and cyclists are also not adequately catered for. There is a lack of multiple modes of transport in the city, and road transport cannot be effective with bad roads. Most roads in the city are not in the best of condition as a result of the poor maintenance culture and poor workmanship by some contractors; the likelihood of accidents increases exponentially on roads riddled with potholes.

Ineffective planning schemes as a result of staffing deficiency of the MMDAs in Accra, and political interference in the enforcement of laws, resulted in disorderly development within Accra and unplanned settlements on the urban periphery.[33] For instance, communities such as Adentan and McCarthy Hill had large areas of their land developed with draft planning schemes, and before the finalized development plans, development had far advanced. This kind of practice is gradually becoming the norm. Most of the municipal assemblies in the city are faced with staffing and financial challenges. This has resulted in low level of community participation in the work of MMDAs. The tax base of these MMDAs is also affected as a result of poor planning, there are many unplanned communities and the lack of enforcement of laws has led to more slums springing up. The most worrisome issue is development in flood prone areas, major drainage ways, areas reserved for open space and future roads. The boldness with which people build without land titles and development permits shows the extent of the lawlessness in the city.[34] The unfamiliarity of the National Building Regulations, 1996 LI 1630, by some professionals of the built environment, is also an issue. For instance, permission is not sought from MMDAs before extensions are made to existing buildings.[35] There is also the desire of property developers to unlawfully use every bit of land available in Accra. With financial muscle, they are able to get away with many infractions. As a result of the zoning and building codes not being strictly enforced in Accra to maintain an orderly character and ambiance, the manifestation has been a capital city lacking in civic centers, urban parks and recreational areas, and a constant thirst for the destruction of urban vegetation and greenery.[36]

There are elaborate laws, bye-laws, and regulations in place that govern physical development and guarantee the protection of the environment. Yet, these laws are not effectively implemented and enforced due to political interference, poor monitoring and supervision, and compromise by implementers of the law. It is obvious that planning schemes are at odds with the planning laws of Ghana. Planning schemes for Accra have rarely been successful due to the presence of unresponsive, unaccountable, and corrupt government institutions.[37] There is often halted development in viable areas due to litigation and it is a common occurrence for a plot of land belonging to a family to be sold to multiple buyers by chiefs and elders of a community at similar periods. Poor record-keeping and documentation make land purchases a high-risk venture and with the absence of documentary proof, litigation is a common occurrence. Litigation is a major reason why people with the required resources often shy away from investing in infrastructure development.[38]

Housing is also another problem that has affected the city for decades. Middle- and lower-income people find it increasingly difficult to find houses to buy or rent since houses on the market come at exorbitant prices and mostly target the wealthy. This has resulted in an increase in substandard housing and congestion in many parts of Accra.[39] The urgent need for affordable housing has also led to many structurally unsound houses being occupied in the city. No matter how poorly constructed a building is, people are willing to take the risk to occupy it. Landlords have often used that as an excuse to fill the market with death traps. Accra has become a capital where density standards, use standards, and dimensional standards mean little.

Some urban planners and architects are optimistic that Accra will purge itself of all its ills, a view not shared by many city dwellers. The situation in Accra is bound to get worse if no conscious effort is made to undo the mistakes of the past. The best urban planners can do is to develop excellent structural and local plans but the real development of cities falls within the ambit of a lot more professionals, traditional leaders, and the political elite. Undoing the layers of urban ills in Accra requires bold political decisions because the form of a city has a bearing on the form of its social order. In order for change to happen, it is necessary to introduce appropriate, effective, and functional checks and controls—something Accra desperately needs.[40] The injection of rational order into the city of Accra is gradually becoming a nightmare. Its urban entanglement has overgrown, and the political leaders who have to spearhead the rectification process have become so obsessed with winning elections that they turn a blind eye to the spatial chaos in the city. The political leaders of Ghana cannot continue to ignore the problems because the consequences of inaction would likely be too heavy to bear.

Calls for a New Capital 63 Years After Independence

Spatial planning is an essential part of city growth. It is the form of planning that seeks to analyze and influence the distribution of activities in terms of location. It seeks to manipulate relationships between places and coordinate activities between spatial scales to promote economic development. It is also for territorial cohesion and sustainable development.[41] It is basically a vision statement. Plans of any kind (housing plan, urban design plan, transportation plan) emphasize the collective decision of a group of people that then becomes binding on developers, land owners, and politicians. Spatial planning ensures orderly development and economic prosperity through attracting new businesses. The city's profile in terms of demographic data, historical information, employment statistics, and its tax base are all factored in the vision statement. The

Spatial Development Framework outlines how key elements such as land use, agriculture, parks and open spaces, housing, tourism, economic development, and hazard mitigation are addressed. In modern cities, through spatial planning, key elements like factories, farms, refineries, airports, and rail terminals are moved away from the core of the city, while entertainment facilities, hospitals, schools, and residential facilities are kept within the city limits.[42]

Since Ghana's independence, economic planning has taken center stage over spatial planning instead of the two moving in tandem.[43] Cities have grown without balance and have become chaotic and disjointed in nature with respect to amenities and resource provision. The three main economic development plans from 1951 to 1959, 1959 to 1964, and 1964 to 1970 that resulted total expenditure of over 475 million pounds, have been the most influential in the country to date.[44] It was through these plans that Ghana executed the Volta Scheme and the Port of Tema. This is a testament to the fact that any investment into infrastructure without urban design and masterplans may affect the revenue stream target or projections for economic development.

The top advisory body on development planning in Ghana is the National Development Planning Commission. Questions have been raised about the centralized planning model, but the balance between economic planning and spatial planning has to be achieved regardless, and a new slate is needed to make this a reality. Climate change has made building envelop standards, impervious surface percentage, building coverage, and building setbacks critical in the development of urban areas. Implementing these measures at this stage in Accra's development is possible, but would be daunting. The political implication of such measures will deter many governments

Korle Lagoon, Accra

from attempting it, especially within a four-year period. In spite of the difficulty in taking such a decision, Ghana is in desperate need of a new administrative capital city where density standards, use standards, and dimensional standards are adhered to. An example of a model city is needed at this stage in Ghana's development. If emergency measures cannot be put in place to tackle the planning defects of Accra, then a new and neutral location of the capital city of Ghana will help resolve the issue of inadequate parks and recreational areas, as well as an opportunity for compact, walkable neighborhoods with interconnected streets served by public transit systems to be realized. More importantly, it will be an opportunity for vertical growth and visual order of future development since Accra is sprawling beyond control.

A new capital city may help reduce the overcrowding in Accra, and present an important opportunity for Accra to be rebuilt and reorganized to avoid threat of sea level rise. Urban planning and design professionals, in consultation with traditional leaders, the government, and all other stakeholders, can select a site and develop the necessary plans. The implementation of the capital city plans and design fall within the ambit of a lot more professionals and institutions. They include mortgage institutions, real estate developers, legal practitioners, chiefs, landscape architects, environmentalists, engineers, urban designers, property owners, civic society groups, community-based organizations, and, most importantly, the ruling government. Each of these stakeholders has a unique contribution to make a city successful. Sixty-three years after independence is enough time for Ghanaians to face the reality and address the issue of the need for a befitting capital.

Odaw River, Accra

The Bono or Ahafo Regions present favorable opportunities for a planned city. Kintampo, for instance, is the geographic center of Ghana, as well as the crossroad for traders from the West African sub-region. Siting the new capital in Bono or any of the surrounding regions will present a unique opportunity for infrastructure development, to enforce planning laws, and make use of urban design standards that befit a country touted as the gateway to West Africa. It would also be an opportunity for Ghana to build a resilient capital that can deal with the impact of climate change.

A new capital will pave the way for local professionals, especially those in the built environment—engineers, architects, city planners, and landscape architects—to build a capital city where buildings are designed in context with neighborhoods that rely less on automobiles for mobility. It would pave the way for local professionals to put their skills to good use. Reducing auto dependence will contribute to having cleaner air, less energy consumption, and fewer greenhouse gas emissions, thus helping to address climate change. This will ensure that the needs of cyclists and pedestrians are realized and that public transport is given the necessary attention, with Bus Rapid Transit (BRT) being implemented without any inhibitions. Additionally, urban parks and recreational areas can be incorporated into design while mixed-use and mixed-income housing where the needs of persons with disabilities and the urban poor would be met. More importantly, it will be an opportunity for vertical growth and visual order to become reality.

Fortunately, the infrastructure policies of government such as the development of a modern railway network from Accra to Paga, the "One District One Factory" initiative, the "One Village One Dam" initiative, the building of new district hospitals, power-generating plants, airports, and, most importantly, the creation of new regions, arrived at an opportune moment to turn the tide. The initiatives can become catalysts for development in neighboring regions, which will in the long term translate into economic stability in the northern sector of the country, and curb migration to the coastal cities. With the increased density resulting from vertical growth and the presence of a trade hub, the proposed Accra–Paga rail line stands to benefit greatly from increased patronage.

Future of Accra

A new capital or not? Accra needs to be given a semblance of order in its future development as it is now in the throes of urbanization. An effective solution to urban congestion has been to connect industrial and business zones to residential areas such that a large part of their personnel can either walk or cycle to work, use a public bus, or take a train.[45] Addressing poverty and inequity within the city by discouraging segregated neighborhoods is equally important and an attempt by city authorities to implement these measures will be a good start for a future Accra.

There was excitement about the government's focus on inner cities and *zongos (refers to settlements in Ghana usually in the form of make-shift houses originally inhabited by some tribes from the southern and northern parts of Ghana and other West African countries. They have similar characteristics to slums)* with the establishment of the Zongos and Inner Cities Ministry in 2017. The ministry's concentration on urban regeneration and slum upgrading will go a long way to tackle the decay in most parts of Accra. Authorities must employ smart growth principles to help revive Accra. Smart growth is urban planning that focuses on rejuvenating inner-city areas and older suburbs by designing new communities to have a mix of housing types—commercial and retail units—and making it transit and pedestrian oriented.[46] It has been promoted in other countries and has yielded positive results. Aspects of smart growth can be implemented in Accra to bring new life into the city. Certain measures will, however, have to be in place before achieving such success.

First of all, land litigation and land ownership issues remain a barrier in the development of Accra and increasing the percentage of state land is a useful measure. The nation must invest heavily in acquiring land in Accra in preparation for needed infrastructure investment by the private sector, through the use of land pooling models. MMDAs can temporarily bring together a group of peri-urban landowners for the purpose of planning. MMDAs could manage settlement growth by preparing structure and local plans that protect the agricultural land on the outskirts of the cities and towns.[47] The data rooms of the MMDAs must be well equipped and run by competent planners. Making a search at the data room of the MMDA offices to enquire whether a plot of land is suitable for buying is an important step for people purchasing land to take.

This is to avoid selling plots of lands at locations locally designated as part of a proposed road, open space, conservation area or for other purposes. If it is a building being purchased, checking whether permits were granted for the construction is an equally useful undertaking before purchase.[48]

The capacity of the MMDAs has to be improved through capacity building programs before the benefits of planning can be realized. Staff and other personnel of these assemblies have to be adequately equipped with modern equipment to undertake their work and the information and knowledge required to effectively undertake their works must be constantly available. The MMDAs need to attract the best professionals (architects, lawyers, planners, environmentalist, accountants, and ecologist) by offering competitive salaries and other benefits. Professionals all over the world need motivation to do their work properly, without which MMDAs cannot attract the best human resource for the complex task of city building and management. A good professional team can positively affect productivity, and, as such, innovation is required to generate money internally to keep a team in place and not depend on the central government for every monetary undertaking. Teamwork is equally important because of the different departments at the District Assemblies. The working relationships have to be smooth and seamless. Teamwork must be emphasized and timelines set to achieve short- and long-term goals. An essential management manual must guide the running of the Assemblies. The necessary legal and regulatory changes to support the tooling of staff must be established. Major decision making has to be undertaken by MMDAs even though the power to do so has been called into question. Political interference has affected the running of Assemblies. The debate on whether devolution or decentralization is the solution to political interference must be brought to an end.

Meritocracy at the running of institutions that govern our cities has been poor. The election of the heads of MMDAs has been debated for many years, but the issues at these institutions go beyond the leadership. There are many aspects of the built environment that are technical in nature and require leadership of institutions governing them to have a thorough understanding of issues. For instance, the ministries of Works and Housing, Zongo, and Inner-City Development, Railways, and heads of Metropolitan, Municipal, and District Assemblies are led by politicians without a background in the built environment. Even though the leadership of such institution may be professionals in their own rights (accomplished lawyers, academics, etc.), specialized professions remain as such and must be treated accordingly. In the same way a lawyer cannot become an ecologist overnight, neither can an accountant become an architect upon assuming a leadership role.[49] Thorough deliberations must go into the selection of ministers.

Solving environmental problems (climate change, biodiversity loss, and illegal mining [called *galamsey*]) require long-term planning and public infrastructure must be undertaken with the utmost professionalism by competent and qualified professionals. The built environment institutions must be involved in the development of programs to stimulate infill development (making use of land that can be redeveloped in the urban core), rehabilitation activity, rezoning, and developing unique building codes, developing contextual design standards, expediting permit process, and ensuring that new development responds to the traditional architectural style of the city. In addition, MMDAs must ensure new designs have architectural elements suitable to a location's local climate, topography, and history. This would result in establishment of character and distinction in Accra.

Having urban growth boundaries within the Greater Accra Metropolitan Area is important to ensure compact and contiguous development patterns that can be efficiently served by public services while preserving open space, agricultural, and environmentally sensitive areas not suitable for intensive development, so as to promote biodiversity. Prevention is always the most prudent solution to urban ills. Nipping things in the bud is a difficult proposition for most political leaders. Politics allegedly prevents the implementation of pragmatic and sustainable solutions on many occasions due to politicians' concentration on parliamentary and presidential elections that take place every four years. They will rather pretend to be solving problems to win or retain votes.[50] Very often, an incoming government—after winning an election—is not eager to complete ongoing projects of the previous government. Sometimes the only reason driving such a decision is to avoid giving credit to the previous government for a worthy initiative. Projects are thus abandoned and the taxpayer does not get the benefit of these developments. Finally, in improving Accra, the bad architecture must be replaced with good architecture and historic structures must be protected. City authorities must prevent the building of structures of substandard quality in the name of development.[51] The tourism industry cannot grow significantly if good architecture is not promoted.

Founding a City

Many of the present capital cities of the world are purpose built. Some examples of such are Washington, DC (USA), Brasilia (Brazil), Ottawa (Canada), Islamabad (Pakistan), Gaborone (Botswana), Naypyidaw (Myanmar), Lima (Peru), Nouakchott (Mauritania), New Delhi (India), and Valletta (Malta). It usually takes more than 50 years for a newly designed capital city to fully develop. Building a capital is a long-term exercise. Citizens are generally skeptical when a decision is made to build a new city. For instance, Washington, DC was initially met with reservations in 1900, but it is undoubtedly a success today.[52]

Deciding where to site a new city is an important exercise, and the ancient Greek's cities demonstrate this importance. Throughout the middle ages and the Renaissance an oracle was consulted and astrologers were brought in to help in choosing a site for a project. Elaborate rituals were also carried out before work commenced on important buildings. These measures have evolved into more concrete theories to guide building while taking into account the quality of life and environmental settings.[53]

The decision to build a new capital is not an outmoded venture, even though many people believe cities should grow organically. Building new cities is not an effective cure to urban ills. Congestion, which was the main reason that triggered the need to build new cities, still remains relevant today, even though many old capitals remain congested: Lagos (Nigeria) and Rio de Janeiro (Brazil). However, there is no doubt that the new cities are equally thriving and growing as well. It is always better to have multiple vibrant cities in a country in addition to the capital than to have everything concentrated in the capital.

There are many examples to demonstrate why countries opted to build new capitals. Since March 2015, Egypt has been working on its new "unnamed" capital that lies 28 miles east of Cairo.[54] The China Fortune Land Development Company (CFID) agreed to provide USD 20 billion for the new capital, with fifteen billion dollars pledged by another Chinese state-owned company. Overcrowding, pollution, and rising housing prices in Cairo have been cited as the reasons for the new capital.[55] In August 2019 Indonesia announced plans to build a new capital. The coastal capital of Jakarta is gradually sinking, and the new site of Eastern Borneo has been selected. Jakarta is sinking into the Java Sea due to over extraction of its underground water sources causing land subsidence. Abuja, the capital of Nigeria, is the nearest example that can be studied by policy makers in Ghana. In 1991 Abuja replaced Lagos as Nigeria's capital city. According to the United Nations, Abuja was the fastest growing city in the world between 2000 and 2010, and its metropolitan area is now home to nearly three million people. Kenzo Tange was amongst the team that prepared the masterplan for Abuja.[56]

The case of Brasilia, the capital of Brazil, presents many other lessons on how the process of building a new capital can be done. Considerations to relocate Brazil's capital to an inland site began in 1789. Urban congestion and the fear of naval attack were the most compelling reasons for the new capital. Discussions were continually reviewed for 34 years before Jose Bonifacio presented a bill to the Constituent Assembly in 1823 to get the process started and to name the new capital Brasilia.[57] On September 18, 1946, that Brazilian Chamber of Deputies voted to move the nation's capital from Rio de Janeiro. In 1953 the congress instructed the administration to select a site by 1955. Professor Donald Belcher was selected to lead the feasibility studies to identify a suitable site. A 5,800-square-kilometer site was chosen and announced to Brazilians in 1953. In 1956, with site selection completed, the Brazilian Congress authorized the creation of the company NOVACAP (Nova Capital) to proceed with the development of the capital. The Brazilian government was the only shareholder.[58] A design competition organized by NOVACAP in 1956 attracted 41 entries from 26 architects and urbanists. Brazilian architects, planners, and urbanists were free to participate. The president of the competition jury was British architect/planner William Holford. The international jury included the Brazilian architect Oscar Niemeyer, but Lucio Costa, a Brazilian consultant and town planner was selected as the winner. Costa's selection was controversial because it failed to meet the criteria established by NOVACAP,[59] yet it was striking and aroused the interest of the jury. Costa's layout resembled a jet airplane, with residential and commercial areas occupying the wings and government buildings centralized in the fuselage.[60] Other architectural scholars describe the plan as having the shape of a bow and arrow. The plan incorporated many principles laid down by the International Congresses of Modern Architecture (CIAM) in the Athens Charter.[61] Brazilian landscape designer Roberto Burle Marx planned the major landscaping elements of Brasilia, with open green space making up about 60% of Brasilia's total area.[62] In September 1956, President Juscelino Kubitschek De Oliveira initiated the foundation of Brasilia. The center of the city was built in three years. Brasilia was originally planned for 500,000 people. In 1960 the population was around 90,000. By 1980 the population had risen 411,000 and the city became a UNESCO World Heritage Site in 1987. The 1996 census put the population at 1.8 million.[63] Costa's design assumed all inhabitants would have equal access to facilities of the city, but he did not account for the workers who built the city and would not return to their original state. A slum developed alongside the city as a result of the workers remaining.[64]

The precedent for building a new capital is readily available. There is also the example of Tema. Constantinos Dioxiadis and his team were able to execute their plan brilliantly. In 196_, the masterplan for Tema proposed a population of 250,000.[65] The 166km^2 site for the new city was acquired by the government of Ghana from the chiefs and people of Nungua. The natives were compensated through a resettlement program in 1959.[66] The same approach can be used to acquire land and begin the process. It takes a lot of preparation to get it done, so discussions must commence on how best to fix the situation of Accra and where a new capital can be sited.

CHAPTER 2
CHANGE IN A CLIMATE CHANGE ERA

Perennial Flooding in Ghana

It is an unpleasant truth that the heavy rainfall patterns in Ghana have become a dreaded yearly occurrence that affects many inhabitants in the major cities of Ghana, with the capital Accra being the most vulnerable. Each year's deluge leads to a significant loss of property and lives. Memories of the June 3, 2015 Accra floods still linger, and makes it incumbent that a lasting solution is found to mitigate the adverse effects of perennial floods in Accra and beyond. Almost six years after the devastating incident, no fundamental change has occurred in attitudes, policy, or response and urban dwellers are still at the mercy of nature—even after only five minutes of downpour. Five years after the unfortunate incident, nothing significant has been achieved and urban dwellers are still under threat anytime it rains. The current nature of physical development in Accra does not give any indication of the country's preparedness to tackle the issue. The most recent announcement by the Ministry of Works and Housing in May 2020 for people living in flood-prone areas to vacate was not encouraging. It is even more alarming when climate change studies continually paint a doomsday picture with predictions of increased drought and flooding in sub-Saharan Africa.

Accra is located in a low-lying area, which leaves it more vulnerable to floods, though, that may not solely account for the nature of floods recorded in recent years. The periodic flooding of Accra is largely attributed to the city's inability to accommodate intensive stormwater runoff due to an ineffective and insufficient storm drainage network.[1] Soil infiltration and plant absorption of rainwater, which is essential to stormwater management, is not experienced in many parts of the Accra.[2] The ability of soils in urban Accra to absorb rainwater has been reduced greatly as a result of impermeably paved parking lots, asphalt roads, and the extensive coverage of land by buildings. These impermeable surfaces have increased the intensity of rainwater run-off and the amount of pollutants flowing into urban water bodies such as rivers and streams. Due to the city's unchecked sprawl, the natural dispersion of rainwater into rivers and soils has been disrupted. Rainwater is unable to be discharged fast enough, increasing the likelihood of flood whenever it rains—as was witnessed in many parts of the city in May 2020.[3]

    Citizens might be partly justified in pointing accusations at the Accra Metropolitan Assembly (AMA), Land Use and Spatial Planning Authority (LUSPA), and the National Disaster Management Organization (NADMO) for their inability to develop measures to avert perennial flooding of the city. One must also not forget how political interference has permeated institutions that are responsible for tackling issues of this nature. Even though there are positives to construction being vibrant in Accra, respect for setbacks and coverage of land occupied by buildings is woefully neglected. It is one of the contributing factors for the increased flooding in Accra. Many property developers do not adhere to the soft landscape requirements of their development. Parking lots and front and back yards are often created with impermeable materials (tiles and paving blocks), which prevent water from being absorbed into the soil.

    The first step in addressing floods in the city is a restructuring of the siting, layout, and arrangement of roads and buildings for all new developments in a way that ensures stormwater is managed at

Yawson Residence, Accra

the neighborhood level. Further to this step, law enforcement must be viewed as a very critical part of the long-term sustainable solution to this perennial problem. The Government of Ghana (GOG) must ensure that the percentage of land occupied by structures (coverage) meets the requirements of the National Building Regulations, 1996 LI 1630. Law enforcement has been ineffective and MMDAs are struggling to prevent the rate of development without permits. Increasing the rain absorption capacity of urban soils in Accra will help reduce the surface run-off that consumes large areas of Accra during heavy rainfall. Collecting excess run-off into urban reservoirs is another good option. Permeable pavement (open-grated concrete blocks and special blocks) can be used for pedestrian areas and parking spaces within residential sites.[4]

Again, the Accra Metropolitan Assembly (AMA) and all other Metropolitan, Municipal, and District Assemblies in Accra must lay the foundation for a biophilic Accra (bringing nature back to Accra). Tree planting within residential areas will be vital in creating a biophilic environment. Tree branches, bark, and leaves are known to slow water runoff and the roots also hold soil against erosion.[5] Additionally, urban tree planting, green roof tops, and rain gardens are other common greening techniques that can greatly reduce the impact of floods within Accra by absorbing rainwater at the source, filtering pollutants, and impeding the speed of rainwater travel within Accra. As part of the solution, a robust network of stormwater retention and treatment facilities must be created to help reduce the negative impact of rainfall in Accra.[6]

In consideration of the high rate of housing and commercial developments, the city must consider the use of porous pavements and percolating concrete. This will serve as a better alternative, especially for large-scale surface parking, and will aid filtration of pollutants while helping recharge ground water. Most importantly, land features of natural drainage should be preserved, and development should be restricted in these natural drainage areas.[7] These natural drainage areas can then be repurposed into mini urban parks and recreational areas. To ensure the success of such a policy, strict enforcement of the law must be applied. The lack of law enforcement in Ghana and blatant flouting of laws have resulted in development occurring in known flood-prone areas such as the Airport Residential, Dzorwulu, and Alajo areas.[8]

Citizens can, however, contribute immensely in their own way, by engaging in standard practices that encourage filtration of rainfall at the micro level. How rainfall is handled at the individual residential sites goes a long way to check its overall effect on the city. Building coverage and percentage of permeability, when checked by city authorities at individual land parcels, can ensure reduced levels of surface runoff and promote filtration of rainwater into the soil. These measures are cost effective because they are non-structural approaches and have the added advantage of beautifying the city. Despite the measures known to tackle flooding, the impression has been created by the political leaders of Ghana that they are waiting for a disaster of a colossal nature to occur before they address the flooding issue with the same vigor as an election campaign. These days, everyone who comes to Accra Central to transact business starts panicking as soon as it is about to rain. The speed at which the city gets flooded is worrying and life threatening. It is as if the same rhetoric has been used since independence anytime flooding occurs. Promises are made by politicians to address these issues but year after year nothing changes. The alarming concern is that the population keeps increasing and more damage is being caused to the natural environment, making it easier for flooding to occur. It calls into question the desire on the part of GOG for an effective solution to be implemented.

    Attempts have been made in the past to solve the flooding problem, but lack of stakeholder involvement and the substandard procurement process have persisted. In 1959 Ghana experienced severe flooding that forced the government of the day to propose detailed measures to prevent a recurrence of such misfortune. The Korle Lagoon was dredged to form a deep lake, a new wider channel for the River Odaw was to be constructed together with new larger bridges across the channel to carry the twin carriageways of the Ring Road. The new four-lane Guggisberg Bridge, 200 feet in length, was to replace the existing causeway across the Korle Lagoon. Tenders for the dredging of the Korle Lagoon were received and a contract was awarded. In addition to all the measures, the survey and overall storm drainage problem of Accra was to be undertaken. Then there was the Korle Lagoon Ecological Restoration Project. Stage 1 of the project included the dredging of the lower lagoon and canalization of the upper lagoon, channel improvement of the Korle Lagoon/Odaw River and the Agbogbloshi canals, slope protection to the

Kaneshie, Korle Lagoon, and Odaw River canals and was completed in December 2002. In spite of this laudable effort to safeguard the city, the problems still persist.[9]

To solve this problem, it will require citizen participation and dedication, with responsibilities shared to remedy the government's inaction with law enforcement, especially tackling the recklessness with which properties spring up in the city. There is enough blame to be apportioned for the woes of our cities, but a large chunk fall at the doorstep of the politicians. If the fear of losing votes prevents governments from undertaking policies and developments that will inure to the benefits of the future generation, then all that is being said indirectly is that citizens should think of today and let tomorrow take care of itself. Again, the level of destruction being witnessed is such that undoing the ills of Accra may be impossible to tackle. It may have to take a natural disaster to bring some form of order, and that will occur because nature always has a way of resettling the balance.

If we are to make any inroads in building resilient cities, the majority of Ghanaians must understand what the problem is, how it is caused, and what repercussions are at stake if we continue to delay in tackling the problems head on. If we have not been able to cope with the flooding situation in Accra since independence, then the addition of other hazards such as landslides and earthquakes may cripple the nation. A solution must be found early, not after the fact.

Understanding Climate Change

A recent polling of informal sector workers and professionals about climate change elicited responses that show how little awareness has been created on the devastating effects of climate change. Many educated people are inadequately informed because of the misconception that climate change is a subject reserved for scientists, which indicates a troubling future for the urban dweller. Since the 20th century, scientists have been on a campaign to bring awareness to the effects of climate change. The subject seems technical and appears to be understood in detail by a minority, yet it affects the global population. The people in informal communities who will also be affected most are occupied with life matters. In sub-Saharan Africa, where illiteracy rates are high, there are concerns that enough measures have not been put in place to ensure that all citizens of the various countries understand the basics of climate change, especially when some citizens are quick to attribute catastrophes of anthropogenic sources to acts of God. Citizens must take responsibility for their actions: the burning of fossil fuels, carbon dioxide emissions, global warming, etc.

To appreciate these activities in clearer terms, one must understand the terminologies and concepts. The part of the physical environment that has been constructed by human activity is the built environment. Rapid erosion of the natural environment through human activities has resulted in environmental problems the world is presently experiencing. The rapid increase in population has led to creation of informal settlements, particularly in the coastal districts that are most vulnerable to the effects of climate change. The consequences of climate change for sub-Saharan Africa, including the spread of tropical diseases, impact on food security, sea level rise and tropical storms were predicted many decades ago. There is a growing realization that the cost of building climate resilience into existing development programs is far less than the cost of emergency relief, rehabilitation, and recovery associated with disasters. Cities that respond proactively have more financial flexibility and that should be the model for coastal cities in Ghana.

What is climate change? What specific changes to climate are the concerns for climate scientists? What are the causes? How can cities pursue the resiliency agenda? Without an appreciation of what climate change is and the destructive nature, citizens may not pay the needed attention, which in effect weakens the concerted effort required to address the problem. It is an undeniable fact that climatic conditions vary from one location to the other. Conducting research to understand the evolving patterns is key to addressing the issues.

Threat of Sea Level Rise

To begin with, the momentary state of the atmospheric environment at a specific geographic location is referred to as the weather, and the integration in time of the physical states of the atmospheric environment characteristic of that same geographic location is the climate. The factors that shape a geographic location's climate are the tilt of the earth's axis, solar radiation, topography, and winds. Temperature is the degree of hotness or coldness of a body or an environment. A period of at least five days during which the daily maximum ambient temperature is 25°C or higher is called a heat wave. These five days must include at least three days with a maximum ambient temperature higher than 30°C. Ghana has a tropical climate. March and April are the hottest months with temperatures ranging between 23–31°C. The rainy seasons are from March–July and September–October. October–March is when the dry season occurs and the north-east trade winds (the *harmattan*) brings dust from the Sahara Desert.[10] Countries like Mali, Egypt, and Kenya also have their unique characteristics.

The earth science dealing with the phenomena of the atmosphere with respect to weather and climate is called meteorology. The study of specific aspects of climate that affect human comfort and the use of buildings is building climatology. The range of climatic conditions that demand the least extra effort by the human body to maintain a thermal balance within a building is the thermal comfort. The classification of climates includes cold climates (polar climates), moderate climates (temperate climates), hot dry climates (desert climate), and warm humid (tropical climate).

Water condensed from atmospheric vapor falling to earth in drops is rain. The water vapor content of the atmosphere is the humidity (expressed as absolute or relative). Absolute humidity is the amount of moisture actually present in unit mass or unit volume of air. Relative humidity is the ratio of the actual amount of moisture present, to the amount of moisture the air could hold at any given temperature expressed as a percentage. Enthalpy is the sum of the sensible and latent heat content of an air-moisture relative to the sensible heat plus latent heat in the air at 0°C at standard atmospheric pressure. Sensible heat is the kind of heat that increases the temperature of air. Latent heat is the kind of heat that is present in increased moisture in air. The gradual change of temperature through a wall, roof, or floor from inside to outside is known as thermal gradient.

Solar constant is the average rate at which radiant energy from the sun is received by the earth, equal to 430 Btu per hour per square feet. The electromagnetic radiation from the sun is known as solar radiation. The wavelengths that make up the solar spectrum reaching the earth range from 290 nanometers (nm) to 2,300nm. Ultraviolet radiation ranges from 290nm–380nm, visible radiation ranges from 380nm–700nm, and infrared radiation ranges from 700nm–2,300nm. The radiant energy emitted by the sun includes ultraviolet radiation, visible radiation, and infrared radiation is called solar energy. The amount of solar energy incident on a surface especially the rate at which such radiation is delivered per unit surface area, expressed in kilowatt-hours per square meter per day is insolation. Sometimes houses (*known as a solar house*) are designed to absorb and store solar heat in order to supplement or replace conventional heating methods. As radiation penetrates the earth's atmosphere its intensity decreases, and the spectral distribution is altered by absorption, reflection, and scattering. Radiation is selectively absorbed in the atmosphere according to wavelengths. Most of the ultraviolet rays and wavelengths are absorbed by the ozone and an appreciable part of infrared is absorbed by water vapor and carbon dioxide.[11]

Biosphere is the part of the earth in which life can exist. When infrared radiation (700nm–2,300nm) that passes through the earth's atmosphere is absorbed and reemitted by atmospheric greenhouse gas molecules and water vapor in the atmosphere, the temperature of the lower atmosphere and the earth's surface rises, and this is called the greenhouse effect. The gradual increase in the average temperature of the lower atmosphere and oceans since the mid-twentieth century due to the greenhouse effect resulting from the burning of fossil fuel and emission of greenhouse gases is known as global warming. Global warming affects arctic climate when ice is lost, and loss of ice results in warming of oceans, which accelerates the rate at which the planet gets warm. Melting ice also releases trapped methane gas and methane like carbon dioxide traps heat in the atmosphere.[12]

Fossil fuels are hydrocarbon deposits such as oil, coal, or gas formed in the geological past from the remains of living organisms and now burned for fuel. Fossil fuels release energy when burned and the carbon and the hydrogen within them combine with oxygen in the air to form carbon dioxide (CO_2), carbon monoxide (CO), and water (H_2O). Due to the harmful effect of fossil fuels, alternative energy sources are needed to replace it. Natural energy resources such as solar, wind, tidal, hydroelectric, and geothermal energy that theoretically can be replenished by the natural processes at the same rate as used are called renewable energy. Greenhouse gas (GHG) refers to any of a number of gases in the earth's atmosphere including methane (CH_4), carbon dioxide (CO2), nitrous oxide (N_2O), and ozone (O_3) that absorb and emit thermal radiation.[13] Ozone (O_3) is formed by photochemical reactions in sunlight from hydrocarbons and oxides of nitrogen that are emitted primarily by automobiles and other vehicles. Concentrations of substances found in the atmosphere that exceeds naturally occurring quantities and are undesirable or harmful, and that interfere with human health or welfare or produce other harmful environmental effects is air pollution.[14]

Ground-level ozone is commonly known as smog and nitrogen oxide is the main ingredient in smog. When combined with water vapor, nitric acid forms, which as precipitation is known as acid rain. The colorless gas ozone (O_3) is different from stratosphere level ozone, also known as the ozone layer. Nitrogen oxides form when oxygen and nitrogen in the air react with each other during combustion. Primary sources are motor vehicles, electric utilities, and other industrial and residential sources that burn fuels. A measure of the greenhouse gas produced by human activities involving the burning of fossil fuel is called a carbon footprint. The human activities or practices that neither contribute nor reduce the amount of carbon released into the atmosphere is called carbon neutral. Housing is a major source of carbon dioxide and other greenhouse gas emissions. Heating, cooling, and electrical consumption contribute substantially to greenhouse emissions. The use of cars by households also produces greenhouse gas. For instance, residential buildings in the Netherlands are typically neither equipped with an air conditioning system, nor with other active cooling systems to reduce the indoor air temperature in hot periods. They rely on the building itself to provide sufficient protection against high air temperatures. Higher energy consumption results in higher levels of greenhouse gases, which in turn, accelerates global warming.[15]

Forests play an important role in sequestering carbon dioxide. Depletion of forests is a direct result of population growth, mining, logging, and other development activities, and these lead to global warming. Carbon is released when trees are cut down and burnt as firewood, and the ability of the forest to adequately sequester is affected by the loss of trees. The carbon dioxide (CO_2) level is estimated to have increased by 30% since the first industrial revolution c. 1750. Melting ice is contributing to rising sea level and globally, the sea level has increased by 3.6mm per year from 2005 to 2015.[16] There is an increase of CO_2 in the oceans and atmosphere leading to them becoming more acidic as a result. Acidification could pose major problems for coral reefs as the changes in chemistry prevents corals from forming a calcified skeleton, which is essential for their survival.[17] There is an interactive relationship between climate change and air quality. Climate change affects air quality by altering local weather patterns, such as temperature and wind speed.[18]

The negative effects of climate change may include extreme weather events, increased frequency of heatwaves, floods, and drought, rising sea level, more rapid spread of disease, and a loss of biodiversity. Biodiversity is the variety of life in a particular ecosystem or habitat often used as a measure of its health; greater biodiversity implies greater health. A system formed by the interaction of biological community with its physical environment is known as the ecosystem. The recurrence of storms globally has its roots in the surge in climate change. A violent tropical storm becomes a hurricane as winds exceed 120km (75 miles) per hour. The same phenomenon is what is referred to as a cyclone in the Indian Ocean and a typhoon in the Pacific Ocean. Seismic activity or volcanic disturbance on the ocean floor may also cause a tsunami. The destructive effects of storms and tsunamis are such that we have to constantly be on the alert. Countries like Ghana with heavy concentrations of population and economic activities in coastal regions are at greater risk of the effects of sea level rise.[19] In addition to the acceleration of sea level rise, extreme weather and variable rainfall patterns are new hazards that are emerging. The risks and exposure of extreme weather events will have the greatest impact on urbanizing cities mainly in developing countries in Africa and Asia. Low elevation coastal residents will be the most vulnerable.[20] Arid regions will also become drier in response to increasing temperatures from global warming.[21] On a smaller scale, the geometry, spacing, and orientation of buildings and outdoor spaces strongly influence the microclimate of a city.[22]

Climate change results in the increased occurrence of both climatic and non-climatic hazards. The climatic hazards include floods, wind storms, droughts, fires, heat and cold waves, sea level rise (water surge), and landslides. Non-climatic hazards include earthquake and volcanic eruptions. The potential disaster leading to loss of lives, health, livelihoods, assets, and services, which could occur to a particular community or society over some specified future time period, is the disaster risk. The degree to which communities are "susceptible" to the damaging effects of a hazard is the disaster vulnerability. Risk reduction, disaster response, and disaster recovery are the three main phases of urban risk management. The National Disaster Management Organization (NADMO) should develop flood maps to illustrate the extent of flood hazard in communities in Ghana. Resilience is the ability of a community exposed to hazards to resist, absorb, accommodate, and recover from the effects of a hazard in a timely and efficient manner, including through preservation and restoration of its essential basic structures and functions. The reaction of many Ghanaians after the earth tremors on June 24, 2020, was enough to show how ill-prepared the country is for a disaster. Citizens are reminded of the earthquakes that occurred on the coast of Peru in 1970. The earthquakes and the massive landslides that accompanied them led to the death of approximately 70,000 dwellers and injured 150,000 more. A wall of ice came loose from Mountain Huascaran and moved at great speed downhill toward the town of Yungay, which was buried. What remained of the town were four palm trees and a statue of Christ in the town's cemetery. One cannot imagine an event like that happening in any city in Ghana.

Adapting to Climate Change

A robust network of stormwater retention and treatment facilities is the object of Low Impact Development (LID). Greening techniques such as green rooftops, rain gardens, bioswales, permeable paving, and urban tree planting are all LID inclusive.[23] Green façades are used to describe climbing plants that are made to grow along the walls of buildings to form a green covering, assisted by a trellis framework. The roots of the plants are contained in substrates at the base of the wall. If the plants are not rooted in substrates at the base of the wall but are modular and consist of an enclosed growing medium placed onto the wall surface but kept separate from the wall material via a waterproof membrane, it is referred to as a living wall. It is watered by a drip feed system. If the green façade is situated inside a building (like at a shopping center) to enhance the atmosphere and indoor environment it is referred to as a bio wall. A vegetated surface suits many functions and aesthetic preferences: it deadens and diffuses noise, makes graffiti impossible, cuts heat and glare, holds or slows rainwater, traps air pollutants and processes carbon dioxide, while providing food and shelter for wild life.[24]

Even though industrialized nations have been committed since December 1997 to reducing emissions of carbon dioxide, methane, nitrous oxide, hydrofluorocarbons, perfluorocarbons and sulphur hexafluoride, the result has not been encouraging.[25] Every country has a role to play. GOG cannot afford to spend huge amounts of money on emergency responses as has been the case with the handling of disasters by NADMO. Economic activities cannot be disrupted because of the nature of informal jobs undertaken by Ghanaians. Preventing such disasters is the prudent choice. Even though Ghanaians are accustomed to sea defense walls being built, these interventions have the effect of compounding flood risk, eroding beaches, and affecting wetlands.[26] Sea defense walls are ultimately overcome by nature. The issues concerning climate change, planning, and urban design must be taught in basic and senior high schools to help in creating awareness. This is because it can have severe consequences for coastal dwellers, businesses, and

James Town, Accra

tourism. Evacuating large populations may be a fiscal measure that a developing country like Ghana cannot afford to undertake.[27]

Biophilic City: A Biophilic City is a city abundant with nature, a city that looks for opportunities to repair, restore, and creatively insert nature wherever it can. Climate change and urban heat islands have demonstrated how indispensable nature is to humankind. It allows city dwellers to enjoy nature in close proximity to them. They must make it their ultimate goal to protect nature, so it becomes an essential part of their lives. Urbanization has led to an erosion of nature and affected micro climates. The consequences have been that architects and designers are beginning to incorporate biophilia into their work. Planners and policy makers who plan cities have to factor biophilia in their works.[28] Research has revealed that nature has the ability to reduce stress, enhance positive moods, improve cognitive skills and academic performance, as well as helping in moderating the effects of autism and other childhood illnesses. Leadership at the local and national level is essential in saving our cities from nature loss. Success stories in Curitiba, Brazil and Bogota, Columbia have been the result of commendable leadership by Jaime Lerner and Enrique Penalosa, who have embraced the green urban agenda and valued its importance in enhancing the quality of life of urban dwellers.[29] Heads of MMDAs can also spearhead these agendas.

Ecology is the branch of biology that deals with the relations and interactions of organisms to another and their physical surroundings. Hydrology is the branch of science dealing with the occurrence, distribution, and circulation of the earth's water, especially its movement in relation to land. The hydrologic cycle describes the movement of water about the earth. Groundwater flow, surface runoff, recharge, evapotranspiration, and precipitation make up the components of the hydrologic cycle. Urbanization can have adverse hydrologic effects and urban planners and designers must make it a priority to protect watersheds. Areas along streams, rivers, and lakes must be maintained in their natural states. In urban and developed areas, measures such as planting of trees, construction of gravel drainage areas for runoff, use of vegetated roofs/flat roofs to aid run off and aid building cooling, perforation of lawns should be taken to improve water absorption and infiltration.[30] The composition of vegetative cover, soil type, organic content of the soil, the topography of the area, and the intensity of the precipitation all determine how effective runoff can be controlled and how infiltration can be maximized.

Subsurface areas that hold ground water, and from which significant quantities of ground water can be extracted, are referred to as an aquifer. When rainwater falls on the ground, it infiltrates the soil, plants draw some of this water and send it back into the sky through the leaves (evapotranspiration). Some quantity of the infiltrated water is stored in the water table to support and maintain ground water levels (recharge), and some quantity flows laterally from the soil to nearby lakes, streams, and rivers (interflow).[31] Watershed is the area of land that drains water into a common outlet or body of water. It is defined and delineated by surface topography. Flood plains are the flat bottom lands adjacent to river channels.

In controlling surface run off in urban areas, linear, planted drainage channels called bioswales are constructed. A typical bioswale moves stormwater runoff as slowly as possible along a gentle incline, keeping the rain on the site as long as possible, and allowing it to soak into the ground.[32] Urban Tree Canopy (UTC) is the layer of leaves, branches, and stems of trees that cover the ground when viewed from above.

Urban Heat Island Effect (UHI)

Land Surface Temperatures (LST) modulate the air temperature of the lowest layers of the atmosphere. It plays a key role in the energy balance of the surfaces of urban environments. The internal climate amongst buildings is determined by the LST and is key in determining the energy exchanges that affect the comfort of city dwellers.[33] The difference in temperature between the urban and rural areas can be attributed to changes in the physical characteristics of surfaces. These characteristics are due to replacement of vegetation by non-porous surfaces, the decrease of surface moisture available for evapotranspiration, changes in the radiative fluxes due to the design of cities and buildings, and anthropogenic heat emissions.[34] The urban heat island (UHI) refers to the phenomenon of higher atmospheric and surface temperatures occurring in urban areas than in the surrounding rural areas.[35] UHI results mainly from modification of land surfaces by urban development with materials that effectively store short-wave radiation. The materials that replace natural surface are mostly impervious surfaces (IS) such as buildings, paved yards, sidewalks, tiled exteriors, car parks, and asphalt roads that retain heat.[36] IS alter urban surface temperatures by modifying the sensible and latent heat fluxes that exist within and between surfaces and surrounding areas.[37] Evaporation from urban areas is decreased because of IS and less vegetation compared to rural areas, and as a result more energy is put into sensible heat and less into latent heat.[38] UHI may disrupt species composition and distribution by increasing the length of growing seasons and decreasing air quality. UHI may also decrease water quality as warmer waters flow into streams putting additional stress on aquatic ecosystems.[39] Dark, impervious surfaces of roads and buildings and lack of vegetative cover, lead to temperature rise in urban centers. This affects night-time cooling resulting in an increase in urban dwellers susceptibility to heat-related diseases.[40]

The fraction of incoming short-wave radiation that is reflected, or the ratio of reflected-to-incident radiation at a particular surface over the whole solar spectrum is the urban albedo (short-wave reflectivity). A higher short-wave reflectivity will result in lower exterior temperatures. The urban energy balance is dependent on the amount of solar radiation absorbed within the urban fabric, which is influenced by the average urban albedo. The average urban albedo depends on the color of surfaces of the roofs, walls, roads, parking areas, etc. Dark colors have low albedo while a white color

Osu Oxford Street, Accra

has a very high albedo.[41] Impervious urban surfaces absorb and also hold heat contributing to the heat island effect, where temperature can be between 8–10% hotter than the surrounding non-urban communities. Dark roofs and paving materials absorb more of the sun's rays than vegetation causing both surface temperature and overall ambient air temperature in urban areas to rise.[42] Most of the heat absorbed by roofs is transferred into buildings, which results in adverse outcomes such as high demand in air conditioning, high energy usage, and spiraling utility costs. Moreover, the lifespan of roof materials is substantially reduced.[43] During the daylight hours, solar radiation is absorbed by city surfaces (asphalt, concrete, pavement, steel, glass, etc.). These materials absorb heat and lose heat more readily than vegetation or soil. At night, heat is lost primarily through the exchange of infrared radiation between city surfaces and the atmosphere. The rate of infrared heat loss varies with type of material. Heavy, high density materials cool slowly, thus, releasing heat that may be desirable. At night, tree canopies slow the loss of heat from city surfaces providing a screen between the cooler night air and the warm surface materials. Thus, night temperatures are higher under trees than in the open. In urban areas, this differential may often be as great as 5 to 8°C. The heat is then either convectively transferred into the air, causing an increase in surrounding air temperature or is conducted to subsurface materials. The resulting increase in air temperature will usually decrease relative humidity. Consequently, there is usually a considerable temperature differential between these surfaces and the surrounding air.[44]

Furthermore, urban building materials are usually watertight so, moisture is not readily available to dissipate the heat through evaporation. Temperatures of unshaded impermeable surfaces can reach up to 88°C during the day, whereas in the case of vegetated surfaces with moist soil, the temperature might reach only 18°C. Urban heat island (UHI) decreases the relief available from night-time cooling and amplifies the susceptibility of urban residents to heat related illnesses. Anthropogenic heat, absorption of short-wave radiation from the sun in low albedo (reflection) materials, trapping by multiple reflections between buildings and street surfaces, slower wind speeds, and air pollution in the urban areas can also contribute to heat island formation. As cities grow and cover the land with concrete, tarmac, roads, and buildings, the natural dispersion of water into rivers and the ground is disrupted and flash flooding after becomes a problem.[45] Anthropogenic heat is released by combustion processes such as traffic, temperature control of spaces, and industry.

Asphalt, the material used for road construction, is a complex mix of hydrocarbons. The mixing and its application are polluting acts. Asphalt and other hard and impervious surfaces of cities increase the intensity of the run-off and the amount of pollutants ending up in water bodies (rivers, lakes, streams). This is because, rather than the runoff infiltrating the ground, it quickly finds its way into storm drainage systems that flow into water bodies. Without an effective drainage system, flooding and erosion are intensified.[46] The prevention of infiltration of precipitation into soil reduces recharge, which in turn lowers the water table, depleting ground water supplies, contributing to siltation and water pollution and reducing ecologically important base flow to water bodies.[47] It is therefore advisable to use pervious pavement. Pervious pavements clean pollutants out of urban environment better than pipe systems do for drainage. The majority of pollutants found in urban environments adhere to dust particles and get trapped in structural layers below the pavement. In pipe systems, all of these pollutants are delivered to water bodies where fish and other marine life may be affected. Vegetation usually has higher evapotranspiration and lower emissivity than built up areas, and therefore lower surface temperatures. Air temperatures in parks are typically lower in the surrounding urban environment (park cool islands). Urban parks and green spaces provide thermally comfortable environments and help to reduce vulnerability to heat stress. While air temperature and relative humidity can be modified slightly by large areas of green space, wind and radiation can be greatly modified through small-scale design interventions.[48] Vegetation cools the environment actively by evaporation, transpiration, and passively by shading surfaces that otherwise would have absorbed short-wave radiation.[49] The use of smart roofs is also a good measure. A roof that uses shingles, tiles, or membranes containing energy generating photo voltaic technologies, or colored to reflect, or absorb solar heat as required by the external environment and indoor conditions, is called a smart roof.

Sustainable and Resilient Infrastructure

The operational challenges of the Komenda Sugar Factory underpin a fundamental inefficiency in Ghana's infrastructure development policies, and the premium successive governments have put on the sustainability and resilience of infrastructure projects. The numerous abandoned infrastructure projects (factories, hospitals, silos, warehouses, airports, etc.) initiated by Ghana's first president, Osagyefo Dr. Kwame Nkrumah, and others by successive presidents call for rethinking future infrastructure projects. The uncompleted maternity ward at the Komfo Anokye Teaching Hospital is another example. Even though work is underway for its completion, it should not have taken over 40 years for such a decision to be taken to revive the project.

Sustainable infrastructure refers to infrastructure projects that are planned, designed, constructed, operated, and decommissioned in a manner that ensures economic, financial, social, environmental (including climate resilience), and institutional sustainability over the entire life cycle of the project.[50] The infrastructure agenda of the present government includes the development of a modern railway network, the "One District One Factory" initiative, the "One Village One Dam" initiative, the building of district hospitals, power generating plants, airports, and road construction—sustainability should be the ultimate goal. It is important to make these investments sustainable, especially because of the rate of urbanization in Ghana and its effects on climate change. The need to protect infrastructure from the effects of climate change by making it resilient is equally of great importance. Impacts of earthquakes, landslides, and the extremes of weather—floods, storms, heat waves, droughts, and rising sea level along the coast—pose a threat to future infrastructure development.

How do we Achieve the Sustainability and Resilience Agenda?

Sustainability is a form of development that meets the needs of the present without compromising the ability of the future generations to meet their own needs.[51] The focus on quality, protection of nature, and applying life cycle costing are the sustainability principles. The Development Planning Unit (DPU) of the University College of London identifies five dimensions of sustainability as economic, social, ecological, physical, and political. Economic sustainability relates to the capacity of a practice to put local productive use for long-term benefits of a community without damaging the natural resource base on which it depends, and without increasing the ecological footprint. Social sustainability emphasizes fairness, inclusiveness, and cultural adequacy of an intervention to promote equal rights over natural, physical, and economic capital that support the livelihoods of local communities with particular emphasis on the poor and traditionally marginalized groups. Ecological sustainability pertains to the impact of urban production and consumption on the integrity and health of environmental resources. Physical sustainability concerns the capacity of an intervention to enhance the livability of buildings and urban infrastructure for all city dwellers, without damaging or disrupting the urban environment. Political sustainability is concerned with the quality of governance systems guiding the relationship and actions of different actors among the previous four dimensions. It implies the democratization and participation of local civil society in all areas of decision making.[52]

A change in the legal and institutional framework governing national development is the first step needed to enhance the institutional capacity of the infrastructure development sector in Ghana in order to attract, receive, and manage the level of investment required, to build sustainable and resilient projects under the various development initiatives of the present and future governments. Creating an environment for innovation and a stringent maintenance culture to protect infrastructure projects will also be enhanced with a change in the legal and institutional framework. Laws will have to be enacted to pave way for the setting up of well-resourced regulatory and development authorities with a key mandate to ensure sustainability and resiliency of infrastructure projects. For example, the setting up of the Ghana Railway Regulatory Authority and Ghana Railway Infrastructure Authority in developing the national rail network will help ensure an efficient, sustainable, and resilient rail sector for posterity.

Moreover, stakeholder participation in the planning process is essential. A lot of infrastructure projects do not have the necessary impact and economic viability in Ghana because broad consultations are not carried out before execution. Landowners, environmental groups, religious organizations, civic groups, local government, and district representatives all have roles to play in ensuring the success of infrastructure projects. Government agencies and private developers must have series of deliberations with these stakeholders. There must be extensive collaboration with professional bodies such as the Ghana Institution of Engineering, the Ghana Institute of Planners, the Ghana Institute of Architects, the Ghana Institution of Surveyors, and Association of Ghana Industries on how local firms can best employ the highest standards in infrastructure development. Interdisciplinary planning of infrastructure projects will ensure the best solutions are achieved to make the infrastructure projects survive successive governments.

Additionally, encouraging participation of local firms in major infrastructure projects is helpful to ensure a longer lifespan of these projects. Local expertise will be improved in the process. It must be the policy of the GOG that infrastructure projects financed solely by GOG will be undertaken by Ghanaian Companies. These companies will be at liberty to form partnerships with foreign companies if they lack capacity, but the Ghanaian companies must play dominant roles. A quota system can be used to employ local workforce by international companies which will be involved in infrastructure development, and international firms must be required to put in place mechanisms for transfer of technology. For senior management and supervisory roles, contracts signed with foreign companies should be such that a greater percent of the work force is made up of Ghanaian nationals. The selection of the local firm must be through a fair and competitive process, otherwise more harm will be caused to infrastructure projects.

Finally, improving local expertise in infrastructure development will mean adequate training. Encouraging as many Ghanaians as possible to take up positions in infrastructure sustainability and resilience will require institutions of higher learning in Ghana to offer programs and courses in the subject areas. The technical universities must begin to offer specialized programs in sustainability and resilience and collaborate with foreign universities to help provide the skilled labor required to take advantage of the numerous opportunities that abound in infrastructure development. How can citizens, built environment professionals, and politicians work together to make our cities resilient? The political climate is such that almost everything is based on partisan politics and the two dominant political parties in Ghana rarely agree on issues. For the threat that climate change poses, the poor and vulnerable need to be the main consideration in presidential or parliamentary elections. We hardly see this in Ghanaian politics and the nature of the problem calls for teamwork. Citizens must pay attention to the sustainable development of communities. Location has taken less significance in the purchase of land in Ghana with the automobile giving urban dwellers unique freedom in terms of mobility. Vast stretches of land in Accra and other cities have become completely car dependent with urban dwellers spending more time in mini-buses (*trotros*), cars, and buses, increasing vehicle miles travelled. Everyday needs of urban dwellers cannot be met within walking distances most of the time, and vehicles have largely become a necessary evil. Transit opportunities are also not really effective because growth in most Ghanaian cities has happened organically, without consideration for transit. Planning did not guide the growth of these cities. Transit is heavily dependent on densities and the higher the density in a service area, the more likely residents will use transit.[53]

Young couples in search of adequate and affordable places to live in the urban core of Accra are constrained by the exorbitant apartment prices in central Accra (Cantonments, Labone, Airport, etc.). The segregation by class/income in many communities in Accra drives many people to find accommodation in the outskirts. Transport options in the outskirts are mostly unreliable and time consuming. The *trotro* is often the most reliable source of transport, which does little to ensure the safety of passengers, putting their lives at risk. There is also the risk of pollution. Electric vehicles, cycling paths, and water taxis (a watercraft used to provide public transport) are options being made available in some developed countries. New communities within the urban core are needed. Land pooling schemes are needed to allow for the development of high-rise facilities and to bring order to the city. Healthcare, educational facilities, electrical power, running water, and sewerage facilities are needed in every community and this is only possible if communities are sited close to these resources.[54]

The Ghanaian media has a key role to play in educating Ghanaian citizenry about the future of Ghanaian cities. The distribution of brochures showing images, charts, and other visual materials will help shape perceptions. A powerfully constructed visual argument can get a greater percentage of the information delivery done. Ghanaian cities have become spatially chaotic and urban order can be achieved only through meticulous and rational planning that would include the careful arrangement of buildings, streets, and squares. With the Ghanaian media involvement, as was the case in the "galamsey" fight, citizens will become aware of how to resolve the issues that erupted. Many developed countries have gone through the process of bringing order to the city after a persistence of urban woes. They faced the same problems of sanitation and refuse disposal, among others, that are being experienced in many parts of Accra, Kumasi, and Takoradi. Elements of Le Corbusier's radiant city and Ebenezer Howard's garden city may go a long way to restore order in Accra, Takoradi, and Kumasi. Catering to the needs of pedestrians, car users, and cyclists while managing urban growth and emphasizing respect for nature is important. Building affordable high-density buildings close to the central business district is becoming a needed measure. As Le Corbusier insisted, formal order in city planning is a precondition for efficiency.[55]

Taking Advantage of the Sun

The frequency of power outages in Ghana seems to have dwindled in recent times and this suggests a lasting solution might be on the horizon. The announcement of routine maintenance of any of the power plants in the country raises concern of imminent *dumsor* (power outage). It is apparent that energy conservation and a diversification of Ghana's energy sources is non-negotiable, and calls into question Ghana's inability to take full advantage of the sun in the provision of illumination and electrical energy. There is a heavy dependence on electric energy from hydro and thermal sources, and electric light is used regardless of the weather condition. Demand for glass curtain walls and air conditioning makes it practically impossible for work to be carried out in most offices (without generators) during *dumsor* because of poor ventilation and lighting. It is very common to see mid-rise buildings with glass façades in the capital where blinds have been drawn to exclude daylight because architectural lighting was not considered in the design phase. The time has come for buildings in our cities to consider the local climate in the design process.

Daylight, sunlight, and reflected light, which make up natural light, present reliable sources of illumination and electrical energy. Fortunately, guidelines and precepts have been established to aid in making the best use of natural light in buildings. The most important factor in utilizing natural light is the orientation of a building. Natural light can be difficult to control and may cause excessive heat and uncomfortable glare whenever care is not taken in determining the orientation of a building. Therefore, licensed architects and engineers must be consulted whenever these measures are being taken. East and west façades experience the greatest exposure to the sun and makes it more difficult to shade direct sunlight, therefore, orienting the long axis of a building in the north-south must be avoided. The long axis running east-west is preferable since the solar impact on the northern side of buildings is usually minimal and does not require shading. For instance, having a library in a residential facility oriented toward the north will ensure even light source and prevent any damage to books by sun rays. Fenestration and shading devices are equally essential because sun rays arrive at a building envelope and is transmitted through a window. The arrangement, proportioning, and design of windows in the building contributes to the quality and quantity of illumination. Windows on the north and south façades are easier to shade with horizontal devices, usually overhangs. Windows and openings facing east and west are best shaded with adjustable devices that can respond to the changes in the sun's angle (the sun changes bearing about 15 degrees per hour).

An important aspect that is often ignored is the building shape and massing (organization of buildings over volume). The quality of natural light distribution within a building is dependent on the massing. Narrow building forms with exterior openings are easier to illuminate with natural light than wider forms. Narrow buildings in alphabetical shapes like L, E, U and T are able to maximize perimeter access to natural light. The use of electric light is necessary but must be used sparingly and only to aid in illuminating spaces where the effect of natural light is minimal. Photo sensors can be used to detect daylight levels that will inform the output level of electric lighting needed to create the desired illumination within a space.

Light controlling systems may also make use of multi-level switching such that lamps in a single light fixture can be switched on and off independently of each other. This allows for various steps between full output and zero illumination to avoid over-illuminating a space. The provision of illumination by the sun does not only result in reduction in use of electric lighting, but reduces pollution associated with electric light. The interception of the intense rays of the sun into building interiors drastically reduces the air-conditioning cooling load. Generation of electricity from sunlight has a huge potential in addressing the energy needs of residential properties and offices in Ghana. As prices for solar photovoltaics installations are becoming reasonable, this will positively influence patronage of solar power.

Most built-environment professionals are knowledgeable about the measures of optimizing the use of natural light in building designs and construction, yet their services are not patronized by developers because of the erroneous impression that they charge an arm and a leg for their services. Life-cycle costing should therefore be the guide for citizens who are yet to develop residential, commercial, and educational facilities. Cutting corners will only result in perpetual occurrences of building defects that come with huge repair costs. Citizens must patronize professionals who will make use of their vast experience and thorough deliberation in giving them energy-efficient designs that take full advantage of the sun. Hopefully, *dumsor* can become a thing of the past, and there will be less reliance on the national grid.

Making Coastal Cities Resilient: Elmina

In 2003 Elmina developed the Elmina Strategy 2015, which outlined ways of bringing improvement to the city. The priority areas included in the strategic plan were drainage and waste management, fishing and harbor, tourism, and local economic development, health, education, and revamping of the local institutional and financial structure of the city. Though the plan did not categorically address the issue of sea level rise, some of the issues the plan sought to address are directly related to sea level rise.

The Benya Lagoon plays a prime hydrological function in Elmina, but this has been impaired by the lack of alternative outlets for drains in the city. The marshes and mangroves of the lagoon have been affected by landfill and sedimentation, reducing their absorptive capacity during extreme rainfall. Illegal logging of wood in the city for construction of wooden structures and firewood production for fish preservation has led to deforestation. Aside from the illegal logging, there is heavy erosion from the sea and rainfall, and negative environmental practices have intensified the impact of erosion in recent years. Rainwater runoff has eroded portions of the topsoil of Java and Saint Jago Hills, and the foundations of most buildings located along the hills and slopes have been exposed. The mining of clay to build fish-smoking ovens has further aggravated the situation. As a result, there is an immediate risk of landslides at Elmina's Java Hill and Saint Jago Hill. A large proportion of the buildings in Elmina are substandard and continuous inclement weather may have adverse effects on them. Some of the buildings are sited too close to the coast and are not structurally sound to withstand the threat of the sea.

Coastal Resilience

An effective land-use management practice is acquisition of land and property in high-risk areas by the government if it is a family's land or stool land. These areas are taken off the development market, preventing the future exposure and vulnerability that the development will cause to inhabitants. It also enables GOG to conserve critical ecosystem or natural features and to provide open space and recreational benefits to the general public. In developed areas, the use of wind resistant and flood resistant trees and vegetation, and greening techniques like vegetated roofs will improve resilience. Mixed-use, walkable, and compact communities that rely less on automobiles for mobility greatly improve resilience as it results in cleaner air, less energy consumption, and fewer greenhouse gas emissions.[56] Coastal population growth must, however, be managed because of the risks involved. Coastal living will eventually become an expensive choice. If people do not have an option of temporary housing during a disaster, then homelessness will occur. For example, the Tonle Sap Lake community in Cambodia lives in floating houses and the Uros community of Titica Lake in Peru live on floating islands made from bundles of reeds.[57] Building resilience is still a function of quality of enforcement and inspection system in place in a locality[58] and the Dutch, for example, through hydraulic engineering, reclamation, and intense planning have managed to live comfortably below sea level (up to 7 feet in some areas). They have managed to build dikes and levees to gain agricultural land back from the sea, and have been able to protect it because of their respect for nature and understanding that nature cannot be fought.[59] The Dutch have reclaimed more than 1,600,000 acres of land from the sea since the thirteenth century by the use of polders. The reclamation of land should, nonetheless, be done with the utmost care if the MMDAs of the coastal regions consider it an option. Building up coastline by mining soil from the mainland, blocking river estuaries, and allowing silt to build up, all in the quest to add to habitable land may cause more problems than benefits. Reclaimed land is a risk in earthquake-prone areas as it does not have the same qualities as hard bedrock on land. Prolonged shaking triggers liquefaction (once-solid sediments disintegrating).[60]

The current state of environmental degradation makes it imperative for Elmina to develop a climate change profile and outline long-term planning tools to be used in mitigating sea-level rise and all other effects of climate change. This will ensure that all plans for future development incorporate mitigation strategies in both the design and location of future development projects. The Municipal Assembly must take these steps as a compulsory part of urban planning, especially for development plans drawn up for the different areas under its governance. The Komenda Edina Eguafo Abirem (KEEA) Municipal Assembly can acquire properties in Elmina at the risk of flooding or other hazards from property owners who are willing to sell. In instances where landowners occupying vulnerable areas are unwilling to sell, the Assembly can then make use of compulsory acquisition/eminent domain to purchase such properties. New building codes and design standards must be developed by KEEA and must be strictly enforced. Buildings in a substandard state that requires upgrading or renovation must be permitted only when considerations are made with respect to the new building and design standards.

In addition to these building codes and design standards, it is essential for setbacks of reasonable distance to be employed. This will make room for ecological systems to be restored and create avenues for green and open spaces that are key tools in re-establishing the equilibrium between the settlement areas in Elmina and the vegetative cover. The KEEA Municipal Assembly can equally make use of a "transfer of development rights" programs in securing undeveloped land owned by private people. Such transfers may be particularly feasible for the vast tracts of land that remain available in other areas of Elmina, which are at an appropriate distance from the sea. Hospitals, schools, shopping malls, and housing developments should be centered in these areas to make development transfer a viable option.

CHAPTER 3
PARKS AND URBAN FORESTRY

An urban forest is a collection of trees that grow within a city or town. The care and management of urban forests is urban forestry and the greater the coverage of urban forestry, the greater its ability to serve as a natural air conditioner. They can help prevent depleting water content in soil , filter pollutants, improve water quality, and prevent erosion and flooding when used effectively.[1] They also serve as wind breaks, reduce air pollution by filtering dust particles and pollutants attached to them, process solar radiation, and help reduce ambient air temperatures. Tree leaves intercept, reflect, absorb, and transmit solar radiation. Most of the absorbed solar radiation is transformed to latent heat by diffusion and evaporation of water from the leaves. The evaporation significantly cools the leaves and the air in contact with them while increasing the humidity content of the air. This is the reason air near the ground in areas with vegetation is cooler than that of impervious surfaces (asphalt, concrete, screed).[2] It transforms part of the radiant energy into chemical energy by photosynthesis. Their effectiveness depends on, for example, the density of species foliage, leaf shape and branching patterns. Most importantly, urban forests can sequester carbon dioxide by absorbing it from the

N1 Highway, Dzorwulu, Accra

atmosphere. It therefore reduces the amount of CO_2 that contributes to the overall levels of greenhouse gas emissions. This shows why deforestation is a very harmful activity.[3] When urban forestry is damaged through development of infrastructure, the rate at which pollution, flooding, and erosion occurs is drastically increased. The use of electricity in offices, residential facilities, and commercial establishments to provide cooling, lighting, water, and entertainment systems, contribute to CO_2 emissions. Trees are needed to help sequester the CO_2 emissions.

A park may refer to a large area of land preserved in its natural state as public property or, a piece of open land for recreational use in an urban area. Parks do not only promote public health benefits to citizens, but they may also aid in stormwater management and reduce urban heat island effect. They also protect natural resources and biodiversity and serve as tourist attractions. Developing more parks and making them accessible by foot, bicycle, and public transit to increase patronage should be a policy of the government of Ghana. Unfortunately, in Ghana, the development of parks in urban areas has not been promoted by successive governments. Some real estate developers are constantly on the lookout for undeveloped areas within the urban areas to use for luxury apartments.

Each location within a city has its own microclimate and is unique in its effect on the inhabitants and their sense of comfort. Making people as comfortable as possible with air temperature, humidity, etc., can be improved by every residential facility making room for trees, grass, and other plants. Trees and vegetation have healing effects on urban dwellers. As far back as 1981, a study in United States by Roger Ulrich made discoveries about the therapeutic effect of trees. In his study, patients recovering from gallbladder surgery were observed with one group occupying hospital rooms with views of trees and nature, and the other group with views of walls. At the end of the study, patients with the views of trees and nature had shorter postoperative hospital stays, fewer negative evaluative comments from nurses, took fewer moderate and strong analgesic doses, and had slightly lower scores of minor postsurgical complications, compared to those with wall views.[4] In most health facilities in Ghana, landscaping and tree planting have not been utilized fully.

Plants can affect indoor temperature and the cooling loads of buildings in many ways. Trees with high canopy, and pergolas near walls and windows provide shade, and reduce the solar heat gain with relatively small blockage of the wind (shading effect). The use of climbing plants over walls, and/or high shrubs next to the walls, reduces wind speed next to walls and provide shade as well. Dense plants near a building can lower the air temperature on the outer walls of the building, thus reducing the conductive and the infiltration heat gains. Plant ground cover around a building reduces the reflected solar radiation and the long-wave radiation emitted toward walls from surrounding areas, thus lowering the solar and long-wave heat gain.[5] The relevance of trees to the urban population of Accra cannot be overstated.

The conservation and management of forests in Ghana is undertaken by the Forestry Commission of Ghana. Urban forests and planting are overseen by the Department of Parks and Gardens (DPG). DPG's impact since independence in 1957 is debatable, but it is fair to say they have not lived up to expectations if one analyzes their mandate with what exists in cities regarding parks. After Accra suffered the earthquake of 1939, not only did the Gold Coast government embark on building modern structures to help reduce slum development. There were also provisions made for the planting of ornamental trees as part of these developments because the government recognized the need for trees. They also recognized the significance of parks and gardens to the tourism industry. Consequently, the Ministry of Parks and Gardens and Tourism was established in 1965. One cannot fairly assess the output of the Ministry since the coup d'état of 1966 derailed its work before the military government reestablished DPG under the Ministry of Forestry.[6] For decades it has remained as a department under different ministries. The primary functions of the DPG include the development, promotion, and sustenance of landscape beauty of the built and natural environment with effective management programs, the propagation and cultivation of horticultural products for sale to the public, providing horticultural education and training and providing consultancy services to the Government of Ghana (GOG) and other stakeholders.[7]

The responsibilities of the DPG are immense, and it is fair to question why landscaping in Ghanaian cities is in its current state. The department is to pursue urban road landscaping embodying avenue tree planting, embankment, and median landscaping that provides much needed tropical shade, floral beauty, and to check erosion.

They are to undertake environmental landscape development and management of urban parks and demarcated open spaces to serve as agents for the production of oxygen while serving in their natural capacity as lungs of the city by providing fresh air to counteract the atmospheric air pollution of urban areas.

DPG has to institute an environmental Landscape Planning Program for the study of Environmental Landscape Land Use Policy and Environmental Landscape Impact Assessment. DPG is to develop public parks for the promotion of eco-tourism and passive and active recreation for the general development of good health. DPG is to develop export promotion programs in the propagation of tropical ornamental and floral plants, which are in high demand in Europe and the United States. DPG is to promote landscape beautification of the country as a whole.[8] Considering the current state of parks and gardens, DPG has to be adequately resourced to carry out its mandate.

Saving the Vegetative Cover of an Urbanizing Accra

Urbanization in sub-Saharan Africa is occurring at a time when fertility rate is high and mortality rate low, unlike what transpired in the United States in the late 19th century and early 20th century, fueled by industrialization. From a low of 190,000 people in 1957, Accra's population is now estimated at 4 million. The rapid rise in

Adabraka, Accra

population has resulted in an acute housing shortage. However, the horizontal growth and the preference for single-family detached housing has resulted in low-density developments in many new communities in Accra. The low-density development has not done much to improve the housing deficit in the capital, it is rather having a debilitating effect on the city's vegetative cover. Vegetation has been lost to sprawling in the capital as a result of availability of automobiles and developments are hurriedly carried out, sometimes without permits.

A careful observation highlights an emerging trend accompanying the sprawling problem Accra is facing. Some of the new residential, educational, and commercial facilities in the city have entire compounds (front yard, rear yard, and side yards) landscaped with floor tiles, pavement blocks, or granolithic screed with little greenery. The construction of roads and parking lots accompanying this horizontal growth, speeds up the rate at which the city's vegetative cover is increasingly being eroded. Sadly, asphalt and paving blocks are materials that absorb more of the sun's rays than vegetation and preclude the infiltration of rainwater in soils. This results in a reduction in ground water recharge and further lowers the water table, contributing to an increase in ambient temperature and a decrease in relative humidity.

It is particularly worrying because among the culprits are the rich, educated, poor, illiterate, and, surprisingly, some built environment professionals who are knowledgeable about the consequences of such practices in a climate change era. The increase in intensity of extreme weather (variable rainfall pattern, extreme temperatures) and acceleration of sea-level rise as a result of climate change makes resilience of cities an urgent need. With Accra being a coastal city, such bad practices will not enhance its resilience. As Accra continues to sprawl and vegetative surfaces are eroded, the natural dispersion of water into the sea, rivers, or ground will be greatly distorted. There will be an intensity of rainwater runoff and flooding, resulting in siltation and water pollution. This will contribute to the severity of perennial flooding experienced in Accra.

Maximizing urban tree canopies made up of leaves, branches, and stems that cover the ground when viewed from above is the key to reversing heat island proliferation. Wind resistant and flood resistant trees and vegetation enhance the resilience of a city. Popularly referred to as nature's air conditioner, trees greatly reduce air pollution by filtering dust particles and sequester carbon dioxide by absorbing it from the atmosphere. Depending on the leaf shape and density of foliage, trees are able to intercept and absorb solar radiation leading to lower air temperatures. Research has shown that a single tree is capable of transpiring 400 liters of water per day, provided there is sufficient soil moisture. Trees are thus able to affect the microclimate of neighborhoods positively and create sheltered zones within the urban environment for outdoor activities.

Using green roofs is also an emerging measure. A green roof is any roof covered with soil or other growing medium and vegetation. A green roof created for supporting biodiversity or providing other environmental benefits with restricted access to humans is an extensive green roof. It is suitable for roofs with a 0–30° slope and with roof substrates that are usually 15cm thick or less. Short rooting and drought resistant plants are usually used. An intensive green roof is what is usually referred to as a "roof garden." Aesthetics and recreation are the main focus. Green roofs have different layers: vegetation, a growing medium, a filter membrane, a drainage layer, water proofing, insulation, and structural support. Rain gardens, green roof tops, and permeable paving are urban greening ideas and techniques that greatly enhances the resilience of communities and as such need to be encouraged.[9]

Most importantly, a concerted effort is required to create urban parks, neighborhood parks, and park cool islands while protecting what already exists. DPG has a major role to play and must find innovative ways to generate revenue and reduce the over-dependence on GOG for funds. Additionally, vertical growth should be the solution in dealing with the urban congestion in Accra. Horizontal growth, or sprawl, should be discouraged since it puts pressure on the limited land area of Accra. Landscape architects should be employed to undertake residential landscaping to ensure a good balance between soft landscaping and hard landscaping. Future developers need to consider the future generation in their quest to make use of undeveloped land in the capital city. Enough damage has been done to the landscape of Accra already, and time is fast running out for implementation of sustainable solutions. The government of Ghana can secure public ownership in high hazard and risky sites in Accra by the use of compulsory acquisition or conservation easement. This undertaking will take these lands off the development market, preventing future exposure and vulnerability that development will cause.

Protecting the Vegetation Zones

If urban forestry can play such a key role in the microclimate, air quality, and water quality, why would citizenry allow natural forests in Ghana to be depleted? Ghana is divided into the forest and savannah zones. Two-thirds of the country is savannah or grassland. Mines are sited in the forest zone and it is common for tracts of forest to be cleared for cocoa farms, firewood, and mining.[10] Efforts to protect the forest zones must be intensified but it remains difficult when authorities focus largely on the monetary gains that accrue from activities that deplete forests. Ghana's forest in their natural state is extremely valuable and an indispensable resource that must be preserved in perpetuity. Achimota Forest has been a development target for many years and is being encroached upon gradually. The Atiwa Forest (covering 725 square kilometers) is alleged to be under threat because of a $2 billion proposed Chinese loan to undertake infrastructure development in railway, roads, etc. It is estimated that there is 150 million metric tons of bauxite beneath the Atiwa Forest. There is concrete evidence on the environmental destruction mining has caused in most mining communities in Ghana. Towns such as Tarkwa, Nsutu, Nyinahin, Sefwi Bekwai, Mpraeso, Shiene, Kibi, and Akwatia have long been known for their mineral wealth. Nevertheless, the question remains: How well have these towns fared? And have improvements and prosperity been experienced in community development?[11] There is also the exploitation of mineral resources through illegal mining in riverbeds and streams polluting these water bodies with mercury. Mining sites are not reclaimed, and sources of clean drinking water have been reduced continuously through contamination. Treating water for drinking has become expensive for the Ghana Water Company, especially at a time when water supply has been negatively affected by small-scale mining and illegal mining activities. Meeting the basic needs of a growing population in the areas of access to food, water, and shelter remains a growing challenge for the government.[12]

The Ghana Integrated Aluminum Development Corporation is determined to mine bauxite in Atiwa despite the environmental consequences and protests from Civil Society Organizations (CSOs). It is time to explore other avenues of generating money

Nsuta

for infrastructure development that will not cause environmental destruction. Our ecological footprint (the amount of biologically productive land and water needed to supply the people in a particular area with renewable resources to absorb, and recycle the wastes and pollution produced by resource use) is being affected.

Lessons can be learnt from the experience of Costa Rica. Large tracts of Costa Rica's forests were cleared to make way for cattle grazing between 1963 and 1983. As a result, large tracts of forest were lost. Deforestation and its associated effects compelled the government to put in measures to reverse the trend. It began by eliminating subsidies for converting forest to cattle grazing land and established a system of nature reserves and national parks. The country now pays landowners to maintain or restore tree coverage and also devotes a larger proportion of its land (compared to other countries) to biodiversity conservation. They have consolidated their parks and reserves into eight distinct zoned mega reserves with each reserve containing a protected inner core surrounded by two buffer zones. Local and indigenous people are able to use specific areas of the zones for sustainable logging, food growing, cattle grazing, hunting, fishing, and eco-tourism. The goal is to make sustaining forests profitable. Costa Rica has gone from having one of the world's highest deforestation rates to one of the lowest.[13]

There is an abundance of professionals in Ghana who are capable of laying out plans and policies to preserve our forests. The Ashanti tribe in Ghana, for instance, have been known to value forests. R.S. Rattray was in awe of the way Ashanti medicine men strove to know every plant, animal, and insect in their forests by name. They were able to "read" the forest as a complex and unfolding document. The Ashanti's understood the spiritual properties of each plant, animal, and insect.[14] There are many dimensions to the relevance of forests and as such they must be guarded religiously.

Avoiding Extinction

Forests are a source of medicine and food; Keeping them in their natural state helps prevent extinction of important plant and animal species. According to biologists, species extinction falls into three distinct categories. First, local extinction occurs when species are no longer in an area once inhabited but still found elsewhere in the world. Most local extinctions involve losses of one or more species populations. Second, ecological extinction occurs when so few members of species are left that it can no longer play its ecological roles in the biological communities where it is found. Third, biological extinction is where a species is no longer found anywhere on the earth. Biological extinction is forever and represents a loss of natural capital. Biologists classify species close to biological extinction as either endangered or threatened. An endangered species has so few surviving species that it could soon become extinct over all or most of its natural habitat, and is likely to disappear. A threatened or vulnerable species is one where the species remain in abundance in its natural range, but rate of decline means it is likely to be endangered in the near future.[15] Protecting the vegetative zones must become a priority for the political leaders of Ghana.

CHAPTER 4
A RELOOK AT THE TRANSPORTATION MODES

The benefits of the automobile to humankind cannot be overstated. For many, it has made dreams possible and opened up areas previously inaccessible. However, in reaping its benefits, humans have failed to take the necessary precautions. It is ironic that a car made it possible for families to escape the pollution in central cities all over the world but today it contributes immensely to pollution. It has also been pivotal in the surge in urban sprawl and resultant lifestyle changes.[1] For instance, the poor nature of roads in Ghana has led to a rise in road accidents, with many lives at risk every day. National lockdowns necessitated by the outbreak of COVID-19 highlighted the detrimental effects of automobiles on air quality and general quality of life in cities. Vehicles were parked, previously bustling city streets became deserted, and this led to a reduction in emissions and pollutants resulting from burning of fossil fuels. Walking surged

Trotro Station, Accra

and air quality drastically improved. This scenario emphasizes the balance that is needed for the different modes of transportation, to ensure cleaner air even after COVID-19. Many citizens now understand the need for alternative forms of transport and how our cities should be designed going forward. Post COVID-19, there is the tendency for people to avoid the use of public transport in fear of being infected by another disease. If citizens opt for walking and cycling, it will be an ideal situation but if private cars (that use combustion fuel) become the option, then congestion and pollution will be back to wreak havoc on an already fragile state.[2]

The world is bracing itself for electric cars to solve the pollution issue, but these cars will still cause traffic congestion. Aside from that, electric cars are expensive and beyond the budget of most Ghanaian citizens, and their use may do little to wipe out the traffic offences many Ghanaians have become accustomed to. It is good the government has reviewed its policy on second-hand vehicle imports because of the long-term destruction to the environment and opted for more car manufacturing plants. In addition to this intervention, timely policies are needed to encourage and promote walking and biking in the urban centers, which can be achieved by building bike paths and pedestrian walkways. Adding vegetative element to our street will make walking and biking enjoyable in addition to the known health and wellbeing benefits. An intelligent application of legislation and planning can go a long way to change current trends in Ghana.[3] We have also witnessed a surge in the patronage of Okada (motor bikes) as a result of traffic congestion in major cities. People recognize the dangers of the Okada but still patronize them to avoid spending long hours in traffic. The Okada phenomenon is enough to remind the government that overreliance on cars as a preferred means of transportation, especially in cities, needs to change.

There are also the mobility barriers for the elderly, children, and people with disabilities who may not be able to drive but do not have access to public transport and other modes of transportation in the sprawling neighborhoods. The high dependence on the automobile in the sprawling cities is thus a major concern. New neighborhoods created by developers must be walkable, accessible, and safe, with the provision of public transport options, recreational facilities, and, most importantly, green spaces.[4] Situating community facilities (library, clinic, police station, fire station, and shopping centers) near residential developments can have many health benefits for the elderly, children, and people with disabilities. This ensures that people can live comfortably without being heavily dependent on a vehicle for their day-to-day activities.

The road classification and circulation access have been problematic because of the situation where development precedes planning in Ghana. In an ideal situation, the effective uses of different road types help with the movement of traffic, but this is absent in most of the cities in Ghana. The basic type of road is called the access or local road. It provides direct access to groups of residential plots. It is purely local in character and has a car circulation access of 40kmph, and a maximum grade of 6%. There is also the distributor or collector road that takes off from the arterials to residential/neighborhood areas. They are the major local routes on which buses travel and have a circulation access speed of 48kmph and a maximum grade of 5%. There are major arterials and minor arterials. The major arterial is an extension of the trunk (inner-city) road system carrying traffic to and from the central business district or other such district-generating traffic. Direct access to and from plots is through service roads. The circulation access speed is 56–72kmph and a maximum grade of 4%. The minor arterial is similar to major arterials but without a median. It allows direct access from plots without service roads. The circulation access speed is 56–64 kmph with a maximum grade of 5%. The express way or freeway is the inner-city trunk road system provides through-traffic within the city, and at the same time allowing exits and entrances from and

Madina -Adenta Highway

to the trunk road system through interchanges at limited points. The car circulating access is a speed of 80kmh for express way and 96kmh for freeways. The maximum grade is 4% for the express ways and 3% for freeways. If cities and towns are not planned with the different road types carefully considered, then the traffic congestion is bound to worsen. Some transportation planners have argued that the widening or expansion of road networks is not an effective cure in reducing traffic congestion or traffic density. In their discoveries, more roads built led to more traffic.[5] The quality of road construction is equally relevant in how effective a road network will be.

Many street networks in communities in Ghana are formed after plots have been sold and developed and as such clear patterns cannot be defined. It makes movement within the community difficult. Fire trucks, ambulances, and other essential services are often delayed in reaching destinations to render services. It has also been established that having connected streets in cities helps in making it walkable and bike friendly. The gridiron pattern, informal web pattern, warped grid, and radial patterns are known to improve walkability and biking. In the gridiron pattern, streets are usually aligned with the cardinal axis at 90-degree angles. When the streets are curved because of being twisted and warped to match the contours of the landscape, it becomes a warped grid pattern. In situations where the major streets radiate from public monuments, squares of key landmarks and not to the cardinal axes, it is referred to as the radial pattern. If different street angles are used then it becomes an informal web pattern.

The Revival of Rail Transport

Road transport is the dominant form of transportation for both freight and passengers in Ghana due to a nascent domestic air transport industry and a railway industry that has been in decline for decades. The concentration on road transport has not been devoid of problems. Motorists who travel between the major cities of Ghana (Accra, Kumasi, Tamale, and Takoradi) are bedeviled with constraints (stretches of bad roads, heavy traffic congestion, risk of night travel, and others). Travel times for these journeys are significantly increased due to the aforementioned factors, which are further complicated by the rising prices of fuel. Again, within these cities, large numbers of low-capacity vehicles equally create congestion coupled with unruly behavior of motorists. Exhaust emissions from these cars, mostly second-hand, that use less efficient burning technologies have harmful effects on the environment. The attempt to remedy the situation with the expansion of the road networks in these cities has rarely been effective in reducing traffic congestion. More traffic accompanies road construction and expansion.

This calls into question why rail transport has not seen substantial improvement for such a long time. It is true that rail transport networks are capital intensive projects, however, considering the fact that the Takoradi-Kumasi railway was completed in 1904 and the Accra-Kumasi railway was completed in 1923, an expansion of the rail network would have been the natural expectation. By 1961, there were daily passenger train services on the triangular Accra-Kumasi-Takoradi line and a night sleeper service between Takoradi and Kumasi. A return to an active rail sector is desperately needed, and the establishment of the Ministry of Railway Development in 2017 came at an opportune time and improvement is slowly being realized. The rail sector will take the burden off the road network in Ghana and ensure longer lifespans of newly constructed roads.

The benefits of rail transport will be huge for Ghana. Rail transport will offer a unique approach to stimulating economic growth in deprived communities in Ghana. There will be huge employment opportunities for both skilled and unskilled workers in rail construction and its related services. Embarking on an extensive rail development project is a prerequisite for the industrial overhaul that the government of Ghana seeks to achieve. The Ghana Railways masterplan outlines the phases of expansion of new rail lines and this should serve as a guide in siting the factories in the

Rail Yard, Takoradi

Rail Rehabilitation Works, Tarkwa

"One District One Factory" Program. Bringing in raw materials and transporting finished products from these factories to different parts of Ghana and beyond will require an efficient rail system since it is a more economical option for freight transport. Towns like Yendi in the Yendi District, Buipe in the Central Gonja District, Jirapa in the Jirapa District, Yapei in the Central Gonja District, and Nkwanta in the Nkwanta South District will all be traversed by the proposed railway lines. The presence of iron ore deposits, high cassava yield, and cotton production at Yendi makes it an ideal location for textile, ironmongery, and cassava processing factories. Buipe has limestone deposits, an important raw material for a ceramic and earthenware industries, and Kenaf fiber, an important raw material for the textile industry is cultivated in Yapei. Jirapa is also noted for livestock and cotton, which makes setting up a textile, leather, or a food processing factory ideal. The tourist industry will also be improved with the rail development. Tourist sites in remote locations will become accessible with the development of the rail lines.

There are measures that have to be put in place to ensure the success of the rail industry. Due to the expected springing up of new towns along the proposed railways, and the towns at the center of rail activity, it is important to develop detailed planning schemes to ensure optimal use of the rail lines. Having masterplans for these towns will ensure orderly growth and improve the economic profile of these towns to attract further infrastructure development. To improve the viability of passenger rail transport, new towns would have to be designed and developed to be less reliant on automobile for movement of inhabitants within the town and to neighboring towns. Congregating housing, offices, commercial facilities, and other activities around railway stations will improve patronage. Regulating densities is an essential developmental tool for the railway. Multi-family mid-rise apartments in close proximity to the rail is preferable to single-family detached housing.

This will require deliberation with local government, residents of communities, and other key stakeholders to ensure that land is made available for infrastructure projects. Land use regulations in the form of zoning, urban design, and land banking measures would have to be completed as soon as possible. The acquisition of land and property in close proximity to the rail lines is a good land management technique for the government of Ghana. Public ownership means that these lands would be taken off the development market, preventing haphazard development by private developers. The success of the railway transport will therefore require active participation of community groups, civic organizations, local government officials, property owners, bankers, and all professionals in infrastructure development.

Lastly, the comfort of passengers is important: having ample leg room and comfortable seats will encourage ridership. Rail transport can compete well with road transport if comfort is guaranteed, in addition to reduced travel time.[6]

Toward a Vibrant Ghanaian Railway Sector

The establishment of a Ministry (Ministry of Railways Development) dedicated to the development of railways in February 2017 by the president of Ghana, His Excellency Nana Addo Dankwa Akufo-Addo was enthusiastically welcomed by all stakeholders in the transportation industry and Ghanaians in general. For the older generation of Ghanaians, who had experienced a vibrant rail sector in the 20th century when the Ghana Railway Corporation was running efficiently, this step by the president was long overdue. Four and a half years after the Ministry's establishment, the enthusiasm seems to have waned slightly, but the truth remains that processes are far advanced in the revival of the rail sector in Ghana. In June of 2020 a contract was signed between the government of Ghana and Amandi Holdings Limited for the construction of sections of

Rail revival needed for cargo transport

the Western Railway Line from Takoradi to Huni Valley. It presents hope that the railway industry will be vibrant again soon; it may take longer than expected but there is hope. The rail industry commenced when the Sekondi-Tarkwa rail line was built in 1901. In 1903 it was extended to Obuasi and finally to Kumasi in 1904. Until the railway's decline in 1973 it transported 1.822 million tonnes of freight and 8.155 million passengers across the various rail lines. The level of decay experienced over the years in the rail sector in Ghana has necessitated a more elaborate approach to reversing the trend. This requires changes in the legal and institutional frameworks governing the sector, as well as meticulous negotiations and procurement processes for the various rail lines of the Ghana Railway Masterplan to ensure the success of the public and private partnerships that are key in undertaking such a capital-intensive venture.

In order to guarantee a vibrant and efficient rail sector in Ghana the highest engineering standards are required. This has been a priority amongst the leadership and management of the Ministry of Railways Development and its agencies, the Ghana Railway Development Authority, and the Ghana Railway Company to bring the most value for money spent. In tandem with the construction of the rail lines, the Ministry has proposals in place to develop masterplans for all the towns along and near the new railway lines. The associated infrastructure that will accompany the rail lines is of utmost importance. The program, known as the "Stations to Cities" initiative will pave the way for local professionals of the built environment—engineers, architects, city planners, and landscape architects—to build towns where buildings are designed in context and neighborhoods rely more on mass transit for mobility. It is government policy that all new rail lines to be constructed will be standard gauge (SG) with a diameter of 1,435mm. These projects are not the rehabilitation works of some existing narrow gauge (NG) rail lines, which have a diameter of 1,067mm. Work is almost complete on the 85km Tema-Akosombo SG line as part of the multimodal transport system. A bridge will be constructed across the Volta Lake to make way for a container port at Mpakadan. Construction work is ongoing on the 22km Kojokrom-Eshiem (SG) line of the Western Line. With respect to the existing NG lines, the rehabilitation works on the Takoradi-Tarkwa section of the Western Line has been completed. The rehabilitation works of the Accra-Nsawam NG section of the Eastern Line has also been completed.

The once defunct railway training school at Essikado has been rehabilitated. Reviving the Railway Training School was at the top on the list of priorities for the Ministry of Railways Development (MORD). MORD and the George Grant University of Mines and Technology have signed a Memorandum of Understanding (MOU) to begin offering Rail Transport and Engineering courses at the Railway Training School. This measure will guarantee that the technical know-how needed to construct, maintain, and run the rail lines will be available locally. These international courses to be offered by the school will bring many local professionals to speak on the current trends in rail development. This will encourage many Ghanaians interested to enroll and acquire certified knowledge and skills in railway-related services. Those who have had training can then become trainers of trainees, including staff members.

It is understandable that a section of the public will be doubtful of the realization of the priority rail projects as promised. There must be a fair process in the award of contracts for the building of the Eastern Line, Central line, and Central Spine Line. We must, however, not lose sight of the fact that the development of the National Rail Network is in itself a mega construction project, one that will need more than a four-year political term to accomplish, and will have a huge impact on Ghana's economy. It will involve the alteration of land through the development of new industrial estates, creation of economic zones, the development of new settlements, the creation of inland rail terminals, and general infrastructure development in many towns. Ghanaians can only take advantage of numerous opportunities that abound in the rail sector if there are enough people with the technical know-how in rail development, and if ingenious ways to support local construction firms and built environment professionals to compete with international firms in offering rail construction and services can be prioritized.

Revolutionizing Cycling

With rising fuel prices and urban congestion in Ghana's major cities, it is difficult to understand why the provision of biking infrastructure is still not a priority. It is more worrying, considering that advanced safety and comfort features, and the electronic motor assist system have made biking a viable transportation option in many developed and developing countries. Biking offers an efficient mode of transport, especially in crowded and traffic-congested central business districts of cities. In addition, it has numerous health benefits. When the state government of India in 2006 decided to heavily subsidize the purchase of bicycles for teenage girls transferring to secondary schools, the level of success was overwhelming. The incentive enabled the girls to travel several kilometers to school and the graduating rates of girls increased remarkably.

Encouraging cycling reduces overcrowding on buses and trains during pandemic periods, as has been witnessed by the COVID-19 outbreak and the lockdown that followed in many countries. Social distancing brings many challenges. Some cities have taken advantage of the pandemic to increase bike lanes and widen pedestrian walkways.[7] Planning for a bike lane in Ghana should not be a question of if, but how soon it can be incorporated into urban living. Patronage in Ghana is low among the middle class. Bicycle racks are rarely seen in office buildings, high schools, universities, restaurants, malls, and many other civic centers. Bicycle renting services are also very rare in the major cities. Most importantly, there is no protection given to cyclists on the street, and city buses are not equipped with bike racks to enable cyclists to utilize buses whenever the need arises. The car-centric nature of roads means they are a danger to cyclists. In spite of all these problems, Ghana's development pattern presents a unique opportunity for bike infrastructure as simple as bike lanes to be introduced on new roads. There is the likelihood that failure to introduce the culture of cycling in the next few years would make implementation at a later stage extremely costly and complicated.

The Netherlands is one of the most prominent countries to utilize cycling as an alternative means of transport. Due to the persuasive

Foot bridge, Adenta

nature of the social movements during Middle East Oil crisis in 1973, Dutch urban planners started to depart from the car-centric road building policies, which were being pursued throughout North America at the time. They built a vast network of cycling paths to make cycling safer and more appealing. Local authorities invested heavily in cycling transport and played a key role in encouraging the use of bikes as a major means of transport. Children in the Netherlands learn how to ride bicycles at a very early age through cycling proficiency lessons, which are a compulsory part of the Dutch school curriculum. In addition, all schools have places to park bikes, and at some schools as many as 90% of students cycle to class. Bicycle parking facilities are also provided outside office buildings and shopping centers, thereby encouraging its use as a primary mode of transportation.[8] Copenhagen has 375km of bicycle tracks. Traffic lights are programmed to favor the cyclist during rush hour. The value placed on cycling makes people feel safe to ride their bikes.[9]

The way forward for Ghana to improve cycling is to learn from the Dutch and other Scandinavian countries. Most parts of Ghana remain under-developed and are bereft of first-class roads. This presents an opportunity for the Ministry of Roads and Highways to consider bike lanes in all new road constructions. Independent bike infrastructure like bridges and elevated bike lanes can be introduced in the major cities where development is advanced. To ensure a rapid and widespread adoption of bicycles, a media campaign can be initiated to raise awareness of the importance of bicycles and to disabuse the minds of the uninformed, of the erroneous impression about social tagging of cyclists. Cycling festivals, annual cycling weeks, and a National Cycling Day can also be initiated to promote the cycling agenda. Aside from governmental action, it is important for urban designers, road engineers, architects, and planners to find ways of improving road designs. This will help in reducing the environmental consequences of automobile use by making alternative transportation modes like cycling a priority in their community designs. In the private sector, developers should make provision for cyclists so that children can start learning how to ride bicycles in communities at an early age. For those who are safety conscious and would want the maximum protection, Hövding, a motion-triggered inflatable helmet, presents an ideal solution. It shields much greater portion of the head and neck and provides a softer landing in the unlikely event of an accident.

Wherever cycling has succeeded, it has been as a result of concerted efforts by civil society groups, social movements, and government support. The government of Ghana can start pilot projects in some public universities. Ghana's public universities are planned like mini communities; as such, primary schools, high schools, faculty residence, student housing, banks, and many other facilities are within cycling distance. Starting pilot projects in these campuses will inform the government on the concerns that people will raise and the measures it can take to ensure successful implementation of its policies on cycling on a broader scale.

CHAPTER 5

ACCESSIBLE AND AFFORDABLE HOUSING

Ghana's population growth rate could lead cities to encroach on agricultural land, since the country's wealth does not provide avenues for vertical farming on a large scale. Deforestation and species loss will spike if cities have to expand and intensify agricultural production to cater for rapid population growth. Growth required for cities should be in economic terms, followed by infrastructural expansion within the core of these cities. Presently, priority should be employment for the youth and health facilities for the older generation.[1] Technological advancement has resulted in the transport of goods over long and short distances by rail, aviation, and sea transport. However, attitude toward physical expansion of cities in Ghana should be guided by the prudent practices during times when cities grew only to sizes that their agricultural lands could permit and furnish the population with necessary food. Starvation cannot be contemplated,[2] and as such, productive land must be protected. The most productive land of a city is usually around its periphery. However, suburbanization of our cities is putting these lands in danger. Prioritizing horizontal growth with the continuous sale of agriculture-rich land for

Adenta SSNIT Flats

residential development must be halted by the MMDAs. There must be innovative ways of increasing the housing stock in cities without losing fertile agricultural land. A national debate on the future of cities in Ghana is much needed.[3]

Housing is a multi-dimensional commodity that includes physical shelter, the related services and infrastructure, and the inputs such as land and finance required to produce and maintain it. Housing also covers the solutions geared at improvement of shelter and the environment in which it exists. The Ghana Living Standards Survey (GLSS 5) classifies housing into eight types: rooms in compounds, rooms (other types), separate houses (bungalow), flats/apartment, semi-detached houses, huts/buildings, tents/improvised housing (kiosks/containers), and other. All the interest, benefits, rights, and encumbrances inherent in the ownership of immovable property that encompasses land along with structures permanently affixed to the land, such as buildings, are referred to as real estate or property. Affordable housing is the ability of households to spend no more than 30% of its gross annual income on the rent or purchase price of housing where the rent or purchase price includes applicable taxes, insurance, and utilities. When the annual carrying cost of a home exceeds 30% of household income, then it is considered unaffordable for that household.[4]

Proximity to schools, parks, and green areas, reliable transportation means, law enforcement agencies, and food markets are usually the considerations made by an individual before renting, buying, or developing a residential facility. Without these facilities the upbringing of children, safety and health of inhabitants, and participation in leisure and sporting activities will be affected. These factors, however, increase demand and result in the value of properties increasing substantially. The wealthy are willing and able to conveniently patronize these neighborhoods because it becomes an investment of great importance that improves their wellbeing and also become a useful asset for their children.

Housing policies are needed by every government to ensure that the poor have equal rights to decent living conditions. Lighting, ventilation, and sanitation must meet the required standards set by regulatory agencies and district assemblies.[5] Tackling unsafe housing conditions and homelessness must be a key priority of any government. The provision of affordable housing does not mean that designs must be of low quality and neglect the wellbeing of future inhabitants. The architectural styles of affordable housing must also be unique to their environments because local climate, topography, and culture are key to successful designs.[6] It is important to factor in costs associated with home ownership. These factors include payment of utilities, repairs of damaged parts of the house, insurance, and taxes, as well as mortgage payments if that is the channel to homeownership. Taking care of associated costs without a constant and substantial income may bring undue hardships to the owner. Again, the nature of the housing deficit is such that no housing project should be abandoned just because there is a change in government.[7]

To improve homeownership rates in Ghana, attention must be paid to local materials. The Ghana Institute of Architects and the Ghana Institution of Engineering must have a hand in the design and building of large-scale housing projects. The nature of the sporadic affordable housing development in Ghana is such that the quality of life of future tenants is given less attention. Mediocre designs and poor quality of construction by political affiliates makes these buildings utilitarian at best. The worst part is their location is poorly selected in relation to transportation, leading to higher costs of travel, distance travelled to get to the Central Business District of cities, loss of time, and increased pollution. Moreover, without government connections and close links with the ruling party, ownership of an apartment in public housing project becomes extremely difficult. If they are not good enough for the built environment professionals to inhabit, then they are not good enough for any citizen. The right to safe, decent, and affordable housing must be supported by the best brains in the country.

The government must find local solutions to Ghana's housing needs. The importation of building materials substantially increases the cost of building. The availability of land and the widespread prosperity of some developed countries, like the United States, allows for the domination of single-family detached housing as the dominant form of homeownership. Ghana's economic situation and land ownership issues may not make it a sustainable venture. An array of multi-family building designs (like a condominium) catering to different income levels can be developed through design competitions by the Ghana Institute of Architects. The Ghana Real Estate Development Association can also input, and, together with the Ministry of Works and Housing, agree on modalities for the successful implementation of different schemes.[8] Investment in local building materials research should be at the forefront of these steps. Publications and media involvement will go a long way to inculcate the habit of patronizing the services of built environment professionals and the use of local materials.

Housing in Ghana

Increasing rates of overcrowding, declining quality of housing, and lack of access to housing services characterize much of the housing situation in Ghana. In many of the housing projects undertaken over the years by the government, only a small proportion of the dwelling units accommodate people in the low-income bracket who need it the most. Even in instances where housing schemes deliberately targeted the urban poor, such schemes remained out of their reach.[9] The key issues and challenges affecting provision of housing in Ghana are land cost and accessibility, lack of access to credit, high cost of building materials, outdated building codes and standards, and lack of effective regulatory and monitoring mechanisms. The generally low level of income of Ghanaians makes it difficult for people to build. The Rent Act also affected the participation from the private sector in housing delivery. When the rent laws were flouted by landlords, their houses were confiscated by

Semi-Detached House, Adenta

the government and these punitive measures served as a disincentive for the private sector to invest in rental housing.[10] Over the years the government has attempted to provide adequate housing, but things are yet to improve. There are fundamental deficiencies with the kind of public housing that have been developed in Ghana over the years. Putting social housing in close proximity to the Central Business District (CBD) is an ideal measure that has not been optimized by successive governments. Play areas for children, mini parks, privacy, and the isolation from the city center and the quality of design in general is always lacking.[11] There is an increase in concentrated poverty in most areas in Accra and the economic underpinnings to support urban life is out of reach for most people.

About 60% of Ghana's urban population is concentrated in the greater Accra, Ashanti, and Western Regions, and they are poorly housed.[12] In the capital, Accra, many households occupy single rooms. GOG interventions in housing are allegedly geared toward their supporters and close allies. The single-room shelters also exhibit the characteristics of slums, such as lack of access to water, sanitation, and adequate floor area. The poor drainage, sanitation, and ventilation results in high incidence of diseases such as malaria, cholera, etc.[13] Kitchens are sometimes converted to bedrooms to address the housing shortage in Accra. Cooking is therefore done in the open.[14] It is disturbing to see asbestos, a proven carcinogen, being used as roofing sheets in many parts of the country. Iron and aluminum sheets constitute 52.5% and 15.6% respectively of roofing in Accra. Reinforced concrete makes up about 10%, while zinc sheets are also used.[15]

Many useful attempts have been made since the 20th century to improve the housing problems in Ghana. The Ghana Real Estate Development Association, Home Finance Company Limited, Bank for Housing and Construction, Social Security and National Insurance Trust, First Ghana Building Society, Ghana Housing Corporation, and the Tema Development Corporation have all played key roles at different stages in the development of housing units. The 63 square miles of the Tema Acquisition Area is managed by the Tema Development Corporation (TDC). The construction and management of the township was its mandate. TDC constructed 10,700 housing units in five (5) residential communities between 1952 and 1966.[16] The overthrow of the Nkrumah government and the resultant financial implications led to a reduction in its capacity to provide housing units. As grants from government continued to decline through the 1970s, their focus was shifted to developing serviced plots and housing (for profit) in smaller quantities. The establishment of the Ghana Housing Corporation (now State Housing Company) in 1955 was for Ghana to have a formal housing sector institution. It was charged with increasing the availability of dwelling houses in Ghana. By the end of 1960, the Corporation had built a total of 416 rental units, 741 hire-purchase units, and 487 units had been sold for revenue. By 1971 SHC had built 6,084 housing units, mainly in Accra. The First Ghana Building Society was also established in 1956 under the building societies ordinance of 1956 to operate as a conventional mutual building society receiving savings and lending to members for housing. Membership exceeded 10,000 by the end of 1960. Funds were provided to members to help purchase houses from SHC or private development. Eighty percent of the total cost of the building was loaned out and repayment was to be done by a term not exceeding 20 years.[17] It later offered mortgages to the general public in a very limited way under the Mortgage Act (Act 770).

Prefabricated houses were also pursued. In the 1950s and 1960s, prefabricated houses were piloted with 168 built in Accra, Kumasi, and Takoradi by the Dutch firm N.V. Schokbeton. This was made possible after a survey by the firm. Their report outlined as recommendation, the use of industrial production methods to meet the housing needs.[18] It has not been pursued vigorously since then.

The Social Security and National Insurance Trust (SSNIT) was established in 1972 under the National Redemption Council Decree (NRCD) 127 to administer the national social security scheme. Since 1974 it has constructed 7,168 flats. SSNIT has developed estates in most of the regional capitals. The defunct Bank for Housing and Construction offered mortgages to the tune of $994,075 between 1974 and 1988 before it ceased operation. Home Finance Company Limited was set up under PNDC law 329 and incorporated in 1990 as a secondary housing finance company and the major provider of mortgage funds for workers. It started operations in 1991 with initial funding of US $23.6 million from the International Development Agency (IDA) and US $7.2 million from SSNIT. Though it was the major housing finance institution in Ghana, HFC Bank was granting about 200 mortgages yearly—inadequate for the housing needs of Ghana. Mortgages have not been very accessible in Ghana. The

Ghana Real Estate Development Association (GREDA) was formed in 1998 as a collection of real estate developers from the private sector operating in most of the urban areas in Ghana.

GREDA was formed as a result of housing sector reforms during the period under the guidance of the UNDP and World Bank. Of the 81 registered real estate companies between 1995 and 2005, 34 were of European origin 14 from North America, 13 from Asia, 11 from Africa and nine from the Middle East. To induce the formal private sector to invest in housing, the Ghana Investment Promotion Centre introduced a tax moratorium of five years.[19] Exemptions were made for custom duties, depreciation of plant and machinery, investment allowances, repatriations of earnings in the currency of the investment, and a five-year tax holiday from sale or rental. Many developers took advantage of these incentives but the benefits of closing the housing gap have been minimal. Some developers, after the five-year tax holiday, ceased to operate by dissolving their companies. The middle class and wealthy have been the beneficiaries of the projects of these developers.[20] There was also a preference for gated communities. Gated communities have sprung up, attracting a lot of middle-class people. Houses are built according to a standard suburban model, addressing the security desires of residents, but cutting out many income brackets in need of housing.[21]

Ghana Housing Policy

The goals of the Ghana Housing Policy that remain crucial at this stage in the development of Ghana are the provision of adequate, decent, affordable, and accessible housing to satisfy the needs of all; ensuring that housing is designed and built with sustainable building principles leading to the creation of green communities; seeing to it that there is participation of all stakeholders in the decision-making on housing development and allocation in their localities; and guarantee that there is adequate and sustainable funding for the supply of diverse mix of housing in all localities.[22] The policy objectives of the Housing Policy 2015 are really elaborate and may be very impactful if applied by successive governments.

Consequently, the following steps are to be undertaken to ensure the provision of adequate, affordable, and accessible housing for all Ghanaians. Prioritization of the private sector in housing delivery via the facilitation to land banks, promoting the program of landownership confirmation and guaranteed arrangement with the MMDAs and regional land-bank registry, providing fiscal and monetary incentives for increased private sector investment in housing infrastructure for those benefitting lower income households, and the establishing and operation of a National Housing Fund.

In respect of rental housing, creating conducive environment for investment is important and necessary. The Rent Act of 1963 (Act 220) will be reviewed, and "rent to own" housing scheme will be promoted. There will be rehabilitation of disused and abandoned properties in collaboration with the MMDAs. Developers will be encouraged to include rental housing in new residential development.

Regarding prudent land management, housing schemes will maximize land utilization. Inner city and urban regeneration programs will form part of the development plans of all MMDAs. The programs will also promote partnerships between property owners and private investors by using land pooling and land readjustment tools. There will be neighborhood upgrading and improvement initiatives to promote mixed-use property development and zoning. There is also the need to promote the acceleration of home improvement of existing housing stock and promotion of neighborhood-level maintenance of housing through community management associations or property management companies. Thus, there will be incentives for the effective maintenance of family housing, and penalties for the poor maintenance of housing with fines and demolition for endangerment to life and property. Building codes and regulations will be enforced to ensure safe habitation (structural integrity of buildings, measures of protection from fire risks and hazards, provision of water, sanitation, ventilation, and electricity).

In addition, there will be guidance on ensuring environmental sustainability and systematic development in the implementation of housing projects promoting orderly human settlement growth with physical and social infrastructure as well as the protection and the enhancement of biodiversity using landscape character/ capacity assessment and local biodiversity action plans. In addition, the Ministry of Works and Housing (MWH) in collaboration with the Environmental Protection Agency (EPA) will reinforce the coastal sensitivity mapping and management initiative to improve information on flood risk and land-use zoning. The policy will promote the reduction of stormwater run-off in communities through stormwater management (collection, recycling, and reuse) for irrigation, watering of lawns, and flushing of toilets, all leading to minimization of perennial flood, and also will promote water conservation through rainwater harvesting, storage, and use in rural and urban areas using appropriate housing design.

The policy seeks to make housing programs more accessible to the poor (social housing) by promoting the use of local building materials such as compressed earth, laterite, bamboo, etc., as alternative building materials to reduce construction cost and improve access to appropriate housing by lower income households. Development of temporary accommodation for the most vulnerable groups in society by the MMDAs where communities and other non-traditional interest groups will be involved in the designing and implementation of low-income housing initiatives. In addition, there will be promotion of community-led infrastructure finance arrangement for the execution of community-driven infrastructure, housing, and urban services initiatives in conjunction with MMDAs, private sector, and NGOs. It seeks to establish a community infrastructure fund for community-initiated low-cost infrastructure programs and support the involvement of non-conventional partners such as faith-based organizations, civil society organizations, policy think-tanks, and research and academic institutions as intermediaries in low-income housing interventions.

More importantly, existing slums will be upgraded, with preventive measures put in place to stop the creation of new ones. Low-income slum dwellers will be empowered to be economically independent to sustain their livelihoods and also participate in decision making. Existing slums will be progressively integrated through revitalization, redevelopment, and regeneration into formal neighborhoods and communities. All housing designs will adequately address the needs of the disabled and the aged. Media sensitization and public awareness programs will be undertaken on the proposed land-use plans of MMDAs to discourage infringements and abuse.

Finally, there will be the establishment of the National Housing Authority (NHA) to facilitate overall development in the housing sector. The NHA will, among other duties, operationalize the Government's Housing Policy through strategies and programs to be implemented by MDAs, MMDAs, and other stakeholders.[23]

The Ghanaian's Right to Housing

The Ghanaian citizen's right to housing ought to be pursued by the government. Housing is undoubtedly one of the necessities of life, along with food and clothing, and all play a vital role in survival. The mental health and psychological wellbeing of a person is equally impacted by the nature of housing quality. It is important that housing for any income bracket or class must be properly designed. There must be a basic parameter in the quality of housing for the wealthy, poor, and middle-income earners. When there is no privacy, for instance, and overcrowding results, children cannot study at home and receiving guests becomes difficult. Without adequate maintenance, children are prone to injuries; damp and moldy interiors are known to increase incidence of respiratory diseases and asthma. Frail and older members of the family also have difficulty without the right housing environment. It is important that housing should include design features to cater for the needs of persons with disabilities who occupy the housing facility as well as guests.[24]

In Ghana, poor spatial composition, visual poverty, and poor quality of construction characterize affordable housing projects. The private sector targets a market where they can make their profit; catering to the poor is not an attractive business proposition. Market forces make it obligatory for the government to embark on social housing projects. Most often, because of budgetary constraints, social housing projects ignore the basic needs of households, provide a limited range of design options, and are constructed with fast-deteriorating materials and facilities. A lot of the existing housing projects need to be rehabilitated to reach acceptable design and living standards. The same layouts have been used since independence without any attempt to vary designs. Same construction techniques and materials are used still to this day.[25] Corruption is also another reason why design and construction sometimes do not meet the standards required. Avoiding waste in the use of public funds is necessary in public infrastructure. For instance, during the reign of Dr. Kwame Nkrumah as president, an investigation branch was attached to the Public Works Division. With the assistance of a police officer of the Criminal Investigation Department, fraud, contract irregularities, malpractice, forgery, falsification of documents, embezzlement, illegal carriage of goods, alleged theft, etc., were detected and the necessary punishment enforced.[26] A lot of savings were made as a result of these interventions for many years.

How Have Other Countries Approached Housing?

The supply of houses at reasonable prices in the urban core is uncommon in Ghana. Some advanced countries like Spain and Italy have, however, handled this kind of situation better. Apartment buildings occupy greater portions of Spain's urban communities. Vertical development became ideal because of the restrictive zoning laws and building codes that created incentives for limited horizontal development. Land prices were high and unattractive. The presence of squares, bars, green spaces, and parks help people spend more time outdoors, even though noise pollution and unpleasant smells from adjoining flats are a common problem within these flats.[27] Denmark also has accommodation availability and affordability issue with respect to housing. In Denmark the average household spends in excess of 25% of its disposable income on housing costs. To improve the accommodation availability and affordability, urban planners have proposed building an island called Lynetteholmen, close to the city center, to provide 35,000 new homes. Twenty percent of the housing will be affordable rental housing for students and low-income earners. Bicycle lanes, a new subway line, and a highway will connect the island to the mainland. The added benefit of the island is the mitigation of the effects of sea-level rise due to climate change, by increasing the land mass around Copenhagen and making use of strategically designed banks (piles of earth) to prevent flooding in the city center. The City of Copenhagen and the Danish government will finance the $3 billion project and 2035 is the expected year for construction to begin, with a completion date of 2070. The Danish have a history of building islands to meet housing demands. In the 17th century King Christian IV commissioned a human-made island, Christianshavn, to be built on wooden poles. Lynetteholmen's construction will, however, entail putting an iron cage on the seabed to demarcate the island's perimeter and have it filled with soil dug up during other infrastructure projects in Copenhagen.[28]

The Netherlands has an efficient housing policy. Municipalities in administering housing funds ensure that different ethnic groups and income brackets have equal access to housing. Homogeneity by ethnicity in neighborhoods is discouraged. Most neighborhoods include mix-use buildings and also accommodate diverse household types.[29]

The Suburbanization Culture Explained

It is the dream of many Ghanaians to own single-family detached houses in ideal locations in urban areas. The problem is that we do not have the resources to make that possible, and even if we had, it would be environmentally damning to pursue it. A country that has pursued it successfully is the United States. About 63% of American housing is detached single-family homes. Many Americans consider the single-family house as the supreme form of human habitation that is integral to American civilization. High polluting manufacturing industries during the industrial revolution accelerated the separation of dwellings from other activities with wealthy residents withdrawing to the suburbs.[30]

In 1933 the Home Owners Loan Corporation (HOLC) was created to refinance loans. HOLC appraisers categorized neighborhoods in all cities according to quality of housing stock as well as occupation, income level, race, and ethnicity of the population. Large residential security maps divided each city into four types of neighborhood denoted with green, blue, yellow, and red color-markers in descending order.[31] The segregated nature of American cities was solidified as a result of biases in lending by HOLC. The suburb gradually became a symbol of prosperity. The highway funds, business tax incentives, and homeownerships subsidies all played roles in the rapid growth of the suburbs. To be in the suburbs was made ideal by the provision of basic financial service, investment capital, and affordable credit for community development. This allowed community members to access mortgage loans to purchase and maintain their homes. This was provided in the suburban communities.[32]

A planned nationwide system of interconnected highways was undertaken by the federal government through aid to the different States under the Federal Highway Act of 1921. Cities that had 50,000 or more residents were linked to the national network of highways. Urban mass transit was neglected. They made a conscious effort to scatter the siting of the research laboratories and factories and at great distances from the central business district. Businesses got the needed incentive in the form of tax breaks to build in the urban periphery and jobs were made available in the suburbs. The

Great Depression halted the suburban expansion and residential construction ceased as well as regular maintenance of existing buildings. Mortgage foreclosures, evictions, and homelessness followed. Unemployment was on the rise and people had to queue in front of soup kitchens. Others searched garbage cans and assembled around restaurants for leftovers and unwholesome food.[33]

Federal Policies and Contemporary Suburban Sprawl

Making the decision that results in the structure and form of any city occurs over an extended period of time.[34] The contemporary suburban sprawl was set in motion through a series of decisions by Federal and State Governments. Federal policies laid the foundation for what has become of present-day cities, through financing infrastructural development in housing, transportation, and industries in states and cities. Suburbanization in America took a different turn after World War II (1939–1945) because suburbs became the desired destination for many. There was an injection of service men who returned from war unable to find homes. Wartime shortages had collapsed the housing industry and they had to find accommodation with parents and in-laws. This created the baby boom and the government had to put emergency measures in place. The Federal Housing Administration guaranteed the bank loans offered to builders. At the time, a local builder could only put up an average of four buildings per year, but William Levitt applied a panoply of assembly line techniques to housing construction. This enabled him and other builders who followed his strategy to erect reasonably strong houses quickly and cheaply, buildings that a bus driver and a teacher could easily afford. Through government assistance, Levitt commenced work on the 17,000 homes at Levittown. The houses had two bedrooms, a living room, and a kitchen with an unfinished second floor and no garage. The Veterans Association (VA) also gave buyers low interest mortgages to purchase these homes.[35]

The federal government built generous incentives into policies that encouraged businesspersons to select suburban locations over urban ones and awarded tax breaks to contractors who built factories on the urban periphery.[36] The Federal Airport Act of 1946 led to the construction of sprawling airports on the outskirts of cities and the National Defense Highway Act of 1956 initiated the building of the Interstate Highway System. In the area of housing, the Veterans

Administration (VA) Loan Guarantee Program of 1944, the Veterans Emergency Housing Act of 1946, as well as the Farmers Housing Administration 502 Program of 1949 encouraged new construction on the metropolitan periphery where cheap land existed. The Federal Housing Authority (FHA) and VA programs helped to support the rapid suburbanization of American households. From 1950 to 1960 the suburban population increased by more than 60% because, with the favorable mortgage loans, it was cheaper to own a house in the suburbs.[37] Good roads, automobile availability, low gasoline prices, and businesses on the urban periphery led to suburban sprawl. A series of federal government tax credit and mortgage policies implemented by the HOLC and FHA favored growth on the suburban periphery over the central cities, and also led to racially segregated residential communities.[38]

Racial Segregation

The opportunities to reside in these suburbs, though aplenty to whites, were limited for African Americans. Federal Government funding, job availability, educational attainment, automobile use, and exclusionary zoning were some factors that account for such disparities. The suburbs were designed to be auto dependent. African Americans were at a disadvantage because they were mostly employed in the service and maintenance sector while most whites worked in the industrial sector and other lucrative areas. Income constraints were a hindrance in the acquisition of cars by African Americans. African Americans did not benefit from loan facilities offered by the FHA. The FHA used the HOLC's rating system to determine which loan requests were to be approved. The result was more approvals for whites and more denials for blacks. Prior to the Civil Rights Act of 1964, realtors had legal backing to refuse sale or rent of properties to African Americans. Many developers, among them Abraham Levitt, were adamant in their policies to exclude blacks from their suburban developments. For instance, in 1960, there was no black resident out of the 82,000 residents of Levittown Long Island.[39] Levittown put clauses in their lease agreements prohibiting renting to African Americans.[40] When the African American middle class became vibrant due to the Civil Rights movement and its influence in advocating for federal policies in education, health, social welfare, and housing, they sought better housing in the suburbs, but the supply did not match the demand. There was minimal public housing in the suburbs and the available buildings were offered based on race.[41] African Americans were considered outcasts in the suburban housing market. Due to such exclusion from the suburban housing market, there was a concentration of African Americans in a few suburban areas.[42] Zoning laws were used to create racial districts that made it difficult for integration of races. Blockbusting and racial steering were used by real estate brokers, agents, and speculators to hinder black suburban migration. The media sparked white flights with their sensational stories and helped to solidify racial segregation.[43] Federal policies have shaped the urban form of many American cities, and gentrification, racial segregation, and suburbanization have been an integral part of it.

The nature of incentives that motivated the suburban sprawl in the United States will be difficult to replicate in Ghana due to the difficult economic situation. Nevertheless, there is the need for effective urban growth control policies. In the case of Ghana, the rapidly growing urban population is not matched by a manufacturing economy. Most workers do not live close to the Central Business Districts. People live farther from their places of employment. This spatial deconcentration has come with many woes: traffic congestion and pollution.[44] The sprawling of Accra, Kumasi, and Takoradi, and the proliferation of the suburban culture are not favorable because of the infrastructure deficits. Family members who do not own cars find it difficult to move around the city, and it is common to see long queues of people waiting for a *trotro*. Suburbanization relies on the automobile as the primary means of transport. Good roads, parking spaces, and affordable cars are the ingredients, something Ghana is struggling with. Going to church, commercial centers, schools, and offices can be difficult and unreliable often.[45]

Ghana's advantage of close-knit tribal communities is gradually disappearing and the attraction to cheap land on the outskirts of our cities has resulted in many communities without essential services, and a higher premium on collectively enjoyed open space has not been promoted. Residential development without accompanying services has become the norm, and land development policies have been ineffective. Few communities exhibit housing with diversity of income groups, bringing households in close proximity to urban centers and ensuring protection of the environment. Ghanaian cities would have to be physically redesigned to achieve such goals.[46] To salvage close-knit societies, planning and architecture should be taken seriously. The character of the built environment should be of great concern to developers. Social concern should guide architects, and a worthwhile design the ultimate goal. Careful considerations should be made before arriving at the household mix.[47]

An effective strategy will depend on how it is tailored to the context of a particular place, be it clustering, diversity, or public-private partnership. An example of how architecture, landscape architecture, and planning can result in fine living environments is Seaside, Florida, USA. After an inheritance of 80 acres in 1970, Robert Davis engaged the services of Andres Duany and Elizabeth Olater Zyberk to develop a masterplan. Construction of houses commenced before the completion of the masterplan. The masterplan for Seaside was drafted in 1982 and by 1994, the first phase of seaside was 70% built. The community's urban code specifies eight types of buildings, sufficient to give architects creative freedom, but equally, ensure the creation of visual unity within the development. A porch facing the street is a common feature of all the buildings, and garages are in the rear of the building. The rational was to have residents become aware of passers-by in the hope of establishing acquaintances. The guiding objective is that everything residents need on a daily basis would be a five-minute walk from their homes.[48]

Making Persons with Disability (PWD) Special

The housing deficit in Ghana has reached alarming proportions (estimated to be more than 2 million in 2017). In an attempt to bridge the gap, a lot of initiatives and policies are being developed. Construction of housing and residential development is on the rise, fueled by the high demand for dwelling units—and although many housing and residential facilities are being offered by both private and government institutions, there are concerns about how best these developments address the needs of persons with disability (PWD) and the aged. PWD refers to individuals with a physical, mental, or sensory impairment including a visual, hearing, or speech-functional disability that gives rise to physical, cultural, or social barriers that substantially limit one or more of the major life activities of that individual.[49] Article 29 (6) of the 1992 Constitution of Ghana states that as far as practicable, every place to which the public have access shall have appropriate facilities for disabled people.[50]

Flats, estates, and many housing units constructed over the years by the Social Security and National Insurance Trust (SSNIT), State Housing Company (SHC), and the multi-family low and mid-rise projects undertaken by members of the Ghana Real Estate Development Association, led to one conclusion that Ghana's housing policies have failed to address the needs of PWD. The Ministry of Works and Housing has not prioritized the needs of PWD, in recent housing projects even though the Disability Act, Act 715, of 2006 makes mention of the measures to be taken. Section 6 of the Act states that "The owner of a place, to which the public has access shall provide appropriate facilities that make the place accessible to and available for use by PWD." Section 60 of the Act also states, "the owner or occupier of an existing building to which the public has access shall within ten years of the Act make an existing building accessible and available for use by PWD." The implementation of these provisions is not being championed though the housing policy clearly outlined measures to deal with it.

People often lose sight of the fact that persons who have acquired a disability far outnumber persons with disability from birth. Aging, infectious diseases, traffic accidents, natural disasters, and small arms proliferation cause injuries and impairment that lead to disabilities of many kinds. Road accidents, for instance, account for many disabilities every year among the youth and the aged alike. Yet, people's attitude toward the needs of PWD is as if they are immune from all forms of disability. So, how can the issue be addressed? Prioritizing the needs of PWD in housing facilities will mean creating an environment that allows them to live independently, through adaptability measures. Adaptability refers to housing design features, which allow the modification of a dwelling unit to meet the needs of residents with a range of disabilities. These include emergency alarm systems, braille and tactile markings, larger bathrooms, larger kitchens, wider doorways, grab bars, detectable tactile control warnings, faucet controls, wheelchair stair lift, color contrast, switches and socket outlets of adequate height, ramps, etc.[51]

Developing adapted housing facilities (housing facilities intended to be occupied by PWD from the initiation of building occupancy) may prove difficult presently, but there must be opportunities for adaptable housing facilities (adaptable housing is used when it is not known who will live in a building before it is designed and can therefore be easily modified to meet the needs of any future resident). It must be the policy of the government to have adapted dwelling units for PWD on all government-financed housing projects. The cost of including accessible features during the construction phase is advisable. Making buildings accessible adds less than 1% to the construction cost and real estate developers must also prioritize the needs of PWD by providing adaptable units in their development. Providing ramps and wheelchair accessible toilets alone are not enough. To encourage private developers to do more for PWD, the government of Ghana must develop new policies, especially in the permitting process for building, and also offer generous incentives.

Citizens who are yet to build their residential facilities should equally consider adaptable units. Nursing homes, senior housing facilities, and retirement communities are not common in Ghana and most elderly people live with family members. Adaptable units can serve the needs of the frail and elderly who require a supportive environment in order to cope with the demands of daily living. These considerations will help relieve any difficulties associated with caring for the aged and PWD in non-accessible residential properties. The National Council on PWD must do a lot more to shed light on the rights and privileges of PWDs. The Council must bring pressure to bear on the relevant authorities to ensure that old residential buildings are refurbished or retrofitted to include accessible design features. Architects and builders have an important role to play by devising innovative ways to incorporate adaptable design features as well as educating clients on its relevance. By so doing, it is hoped that future housing designs will adequately address the needs of PWD.

Housing Prisoners and Making Prisons Model Communities

Aaron Baral said, "A society is judged by the quality of its prisons and an enlightened society is judged by the treatment of its prisoners." Prisons, penitentiaries, or correctional facilities may be considered as segregated cities. Within the walls of prisons, all that is required for the upkeep of prisoners or inmates must be provided. Prisons have been in existence for centuries as a means of rehabilitating citizens who commit crimes against society. But over the years, the high rate of recidivism (the tendency of a convicted criminal to reoffend) led to a review of the penal system in many advanced societies. Many countries have abandoned the crudeness and torment that were associated with earlier prisons. Transforming criminals into model citizens is the driving force behind modern prisons or correctional facilities.

Ghana's penal system is inundated with problems. The majority of the prisons were not purposefully built, and as such are not adequately equipped to address the needs of inmates in the reformation process. Apart from the Ankaful Maximum Security Prison, which was inaugurated in 2011, there has not been any purposefully built prison in Ghana since 1962. For instance, Kumasi Central Prison was established in 1901 and rehabilitated in 1925, while Nsawam Medium Security Prison was built in 1960. Although these prisons represented advanced thinking when they were constructed, they offer an inappropriate response to today's correctional ideals. Currently, there are high levels of overcrowding in a majority of prisons in Ghana. As of 2009 the authorized capacity of prisons in Ghana was 7,875 inmates, but the population as of February 6, 2009, was 14,023 and there has not been any significant improvement since. In September 2019 the prison population was 15,461. There is an unbearable load on the few obsolete, low-capacity prisons in the country. The treatment of Ghanaian prisoners could be likened to what existed in the early nineteenth century in Europe when the main goal of imprisonment was revenge. Differential access to legal representation has resulted in prison population disproportionately constituted by the poor in

James Fort, Accra

society. Even when they have been unjustifiably sentenced, it takes many years for remedies to be sought, because of the financial consequences associated with the fight for justice.

New trends in Prison Design

The current trend in prison design represents the philosophical direction of reformation, rehabilitation, and reintegration. It has been adopted by many countries because it has become apparent that it is not enough to resort to higher penalties, including longer sentences for criminal activities, and expect change in the character of an inmate. Iron bars and concrete walls alone do little to reform criminals. Many criminologists argue that social problems such as unemployment, homelessness, discrimination, inadequate health care, and unequal education, left unaddressed, will lead to an unabated rate of incarceration. Prison designers are therefore creating more humane environment for medium- and minimum-security facilities with the use of softer materials like carpeting, wooden doors, floor tiles, and improved color code for interior walls, better acoustics, and more natural light in cells. Softer materials serve as an incentive for prisoners to be responsible for their surroundings. The physical appearance of modern correctional facilities and its spaces do not deviate too much from what happens in normal life. For instance, in many Scandinavian countries, the interior design of prisons is intentionally made luxurious, and the results on inmate reformation have been highly positive. Attention is also paid to the needs of prison officers and other workers engaged in the daily running of prisons. Well-equipped gymnasiums, libraries, changing rooms, and other amenities are becoming more common as a way to create a less stressful environment for both inmates and prison officers.

CHAPTER 6
SLUMS AND SQUATTER SETTLEMENT

The Issue of Population Explosion

Tackling population growth has become an important measure because of the trends in sub-Saharan Africa, South America, and Asia at the turn of the 21st century. Globally, it is estimated that 160 million people lived in cities in 1900. In 1950 it stood at 751 million. It rose to more than 3 billion in 2000 and by 2018 it had reached 4.2 billion. Presently, more than half of the world's population live in cities and this is set to increase to two thirds by 2050. Around 1900, most of the more populous cities (New York, Los Angeles, London) used to be in Europe and America. By 2000, more cities had joined the list and megacities have become a common trend. Examples of cities that saw massive growth during the 20th century are Mexico City (25.6 million), Sao Paulo (22.1 million), Jakarta (13.7 million), Manilla (11.8 million), Lagos (12.9 million) and Delhi (13.2 million). They have all surpassed the 8-million-person minimum population

Squatter Settlement, Mempeasem, Accra

for a megacity.[1] The West African Country, Nigeria, for instance, is expected to overtake the United States to become the third most populated country in the world. Only China and India will remain ahead of Nigeria. The population of Lagos is estimated to be 14 million by the UN and 21 million by the Lagos State Government.[2] Either way, there is trouble looming. Coping with its sprawling population will become problematic if prudent measures are not put in place. Accra may not be too far from reaching megacity status if care is not taken.

Accra is also experiencing high population growth. Meeting the different needs of urban dwellers within the city is already a daunting task for local governments. Roads, buildings, hospitals, parks, and schools are basic building blocks of the complex network of cities are lacking. Careful and well-thought-out decisions by politicians, built environment professionals, and all stakeholders are required. Not all citizens will be pleased when order is being brought into the city. There should obviously not be any bias toward specific communities, for public funds are used in undertaking such interventions. To ensure that buildings and structures of Ghanaian cities remain useful and architecturally relevant for generations to come, it requires architects, planners, and urban designers to think of the legacies their works will command.[3]

Rising populations may lead to the creation of slum areas when the government is unable to meet the housing demands. Raising children in a conducive environment is the ultimate goal of every parent. The spatial isolation of these communities has psychological effects on children. Poor conditions in slum areas make children without education more prone to bad influence. They are susceptible to gangs and bad company during their formative years. The lack of parks and playgrounds, schools, and safer workplaces, as well as unclean water and air in these neighborhoods, stifle the growth of children.[4] Working to make ends meet may take precious time away from children who should have been occupied with school. In 2020, COVID-19 reminded us how vulnerable the world is to pandemics, and how the poor always endure the most. The wealthy are able to put up structures that protect them from the risk of pandemic, war, terrorist attacks, and nuclear strike. Custom high-end bunkers that can last for a generation, withstand an earthquake, and are able to store food and supplies for a minimum of a year per resident are on the rise. These options are available to a minority, but the lives of the majority equally matter.[5] The equitable distribution of a nation's wealth remains an issue that has been lingering for centuries. How can the wealth of a nation be distributed fairly such that any hard-working individual in the informal sector can comfortably earn a living? This question becomes more difficult to address when population increase is not matched with housing and other infrastructure provision. For instance, when urban growth outpaces the installation of sanitation and water facilities, the spread of disease becomes difficult to deal with, especially in slum communities. Crowded slums without running water and sewers put inhabitants at risk of spreading disease.[6] The increase in slum populations is also an indication of the private sector and government's inability to supply decent and affordable housing.[7]

It is interesting to note that medical advancement and improvement in sanitation have provided protection for many global citizens, considering the fact that almost half of Europe was wiped out during the 14th century as a result of the bubonic plague. The plague was spread by infected fleas on rats, and they spread rapidly. Whole villages were wiped out, the workforce for farming activities was lost, and famine affected many others as a result.[8] Population has dropped anytime there is famine or disease as a result of a reduction in birthrate as fewer people were left in the city.[9]

Population growth also leads to suburban development eroding agricultural land surrounding cities. Food security is affected because food production in close proximity to urban centers is lost. Food importation makes up the difference in food requirements of the population when agricultural land is lost. The distance food travels increases the ecological footprint of cities The energy consumed in transporting the food affects the environment negatively. Labor-intensive industrialization was the major driving force for European and American urbanization. People were assured of jobs when they moved from the rural areas to urban centers. The growth of population through high fertility rates drives the present urbanization in sub-Saharan Africa. The phenomena of high fertility and low mortality rates in many West African countries is more alarming compared to Europe in the 19th century when mortality rates were high and fertility rates low. Plagues had devastating effects on people resulting in deaths, as healthcare at the time was not as effective as today.[10]

Without systematic planning, cities may grow in a haphazard and rapid manner. Without the government's control, the unchecked growth may cause further complications associated with squalid settlements (vice, crime, disease, teenage pregnancy). The construction of dwelling with inferior materials puts inhabitant at risk of fire and flooding. Slum dwellers usually occupy riskier parts of cities like steep slopes and flood plains that are at the mercy of climate change threats.[11] Fire outbreaks, earthquakes, landslides and other epidemics have devastating effect on slum settlements. Wood is the most dominant building material in slum communities in Ghana. The nature of building in slum areas and squatter settlement with wood, scrap iron, and corrugated roofing sheets will not withstand any earthquake or fire. The fire of 1666 destroyed most parts of medieval London; mass timber framed building made it easy for the fire to spread rapidly.[12] An earthquake struck the Portuguese capital Lisbon in 1755 killing between 30–40 thousand people with 85% of Lisbon's buildings destroyed. One cannot imagine such an incident in a slum area in a Ghanaian city.

Defining Slums

Slum areas are characterized by lack of essential services and necessary infrastructure. Slum dwellers occupy lands that are usually unsuited to human settlement (swampy areas, garbage dump sites, sloping sites, and hazardous areas) because they do not have rights to occupy the land.[13] Ghana's National Housing Policy defines a slum as a group of individuals living under the same roof in an urban area who lack one or more of the following: (1) durable housing of a permanent nature that protects against extreme climate conditions; (2) sufficient living space, which means not more than three people sharing the same room; (3) easy access to potable water in sufficient amounts at an affordable price; (4) access to adequate sanitation in the form of private or public toilet shared by a reasonable number of people; and (5) security of tenure that prevents forced eviction.[14] The indicators of slums are access to water, access to sanitation, access to secure tenure, durability of housing, and sufficient living area.[15] A technical application of the indicators will result in a greater percentage of urban areas in Ghana being slums.

A squatter settlement is a group of dwellings erected on land that the occupants hold no title to. The defining characteristic is the illegality of the occupation of land. The main difference between a squatter settlement and an unplanned settlement is that with an unplanned settlement resident may hold title to the land or occupy the land with the consent of the landowner.[16] Many areas in the major cities (Accra, Kumasi, and Takoradi) are characterized by an amalgam of informal and dilapidated housing, disease, poverty, overcrowding, inadequate access to safe water, sanitation, and insecurity of tenure. It paints a clear picture of the extent to which the country is affected by slums.[17]

Even though slums are usually densely population, they grow horizontally and without building codes and land use regulations. Development in slums areas violate many laws and regulations, but successive governments have found it difficult to address these issues, because these areas are fertile grounds for political campaigns. Aside the voting power slum dwellers wield in Ghana, they also play an important role in the development of the nation as they provide labor for most of the essential services carried out all over the major cities.

Enforcing laws and regulations may sometimes lead to gentrification (the purchase and improvement of working-class properties by entrepreneurs or middle-class families in inner urban areas). The lack of tenure makes it difficult for slum dwellers to make the necessary investment. The constant threat of eviction

Bathing Unit in Squatter Settlement

deters horizontal development and puts vertical construction out of the picture. Without guidelines governing development of physical infrastructure, slums grow organically and rapidly, and the resultant effect is the increased congestion accompanied by health and safety risk.[18] Slums are common in Accra, Kumasi, and Takoradi. What has helped to mitigate the proliferation of slums in other parts of the country is the fact that stronger clan ties in Ghana contributes to the make-up of households. The extended family system allows poor people to dwell in family houses with wealthier kinfolk.[19] The same extends to slum dwellings where a single kiosk may be occupied by members of an extended family.

The Global Picture

Some highly developed countries like the United States battled urban blight through clearing slums in the urban renewal period of the 1960s.[20] There were slum areas in urban centers such as New York City. In some tenement houses, there was no light or ventilation, no bathrooms, and the privy was in the rear yard. All the rooms were attached, without corridors, and one could walk through adjoining rooms. It was later that common toilet facilities were introduced on each floor in the public halls. Bathing was restricted to a bathtub in the kitchen. All the wealthy countries in the world have battled with slum prevalence at some period/stage in their history. If you consider Robert Downing's assertion that a dwelling/residential facility may not be considered complete if it has no water closet for use by occupants, then one may understand how dire the situation in a slum is.[21] Sanitary facilities are inadequate in slum areas, a single open latrine may be shared by 20–25 families. It is common to see people defecating in the open and traces of human excrement visible in the open space. This leads to the spread of diseases coupled with the practice of indiscriminate dumping of refuse in slums.[22]

There are probably more than 200,000 slums in the world, ranging in population from a few hundreds to more than a million people. Many governments have struggled to find a solution to this menace. It is worrying that most developing countries continue to grapple in search of lasting solutions to the problem of slums. The issue of slums is worse in sub-Saharan Africa. In 2012, about 863 million people in the developing world lived in slums with 226 million in sub-Saharan Africa. United Nations projections suggest that a higher proportion of people in Africa will live in urban areas by 2030.[23] Rural urban migration is cited as the major factor resulting in slum development. People travel from villages to urban centers in search of non-existent jobs, and upon arrival they face economic hardships that lead to life in the slum.[24]

The human immunodeficiency virus (HIV) prevalence in urban areas is principally fueled by very high HIV infection rates in slum areas. Slum areas are characterized by early exposure to sexual activity. For example, at 14 years, 50% of slum girls have already had sex, and surprisingly most of the sexually active youth do not feel that they are at risk of contracting HIV and have never been tested.[25] As a result of overcrowding, poor sanitary conditions and substandard living conditions, infections, and chronic diseases are always on the increase in slums. Slums have high population density and no spaces devoted to physical activity.[26] Alcohol, drug use, and addiction are also persistent issues in slum areas. The Millennium Development Goal 7 required achieving a significant improvement in the lives of at least 100 million slum dwellers by 2020 by reducing poverty and improving water and sanitation.[27] It has not been impactful in most slums in Ghana. COVID-19 has shown that a lot more has to be done. Hopefully, the sustainable development goals will be diligently pursued by the leaders of Ghana to bring the needed changes to slum areas.

Life of the Slum Dweller

The high rate of poverty in slum neighborhoods makes a pandemic a dreaded event. It became evident during the period of lockdown in Ghana where people were forced to stock up food for the period. The disadvantaged could not even dream of embarking on such measures because they survive hand to mouth. Aside from the pandemic, issues of teenage pregnancy, unemployment, high rate of crime, poor education, drug addiction, and alcoholism still persist. Children are the most vulnerable of all slum dwellers. Raising children in such environments remains a difficult task for parents with the feeling that their children's talents and aspiration may be inhibited. This may be due to the fact that they engage in some form of commercial activity to assist in the running of the home. When they leave rural schools, they miss long periods of schooling before they are able to enroll in urban schools and may be unable to join or complete school at their urban destination. The sizeable increase in rural-urban migration, and the relative lack of attention paid to urban poverty, results in multidimensional deprivation.

Children who live in slums usually drop out of school due to a number of reasons. It is generally believed that financial constraint remains the biggest impediment for parents living in slums when it comes to the issue of their children's education. The cost of education in urban areas is relatively higher and rural children who are fortunate enough to enroll in school often dropout on their own volition due to an inferiority complex. This is largely due to the fact that they cannot compete or keep up with their peers in the urban areas. Unsatisfactory performances in school by children in slum areas serve as a disincentive. Due to the fact that schools are not usually found in slum areas because of the illegal status of the settlement, the schools that serve the slum communities are mainly informal schools. These schools are characterized by shortage of staff, congested classrooms and lack of scholastic materials.[28] The nearest equipped schools are not within walking distances and children would have to make use of public transport, which is usually costly. Also, because their mother tongue is usually not English, slum children struggle to learn the English language at school.[29] Hopefully, the Free Senior High School will be a welcome relief for most slum dwellers of high school age. Policies must also be put in place to ensure primary education is equally promoted.

Growth of Slums

The population of Ashaiman has surpassed that of Tema. The 2000 census put Ashaiman's population at 150,312 and Tema at 141,479.[30] Ashaiman (formerly a small village called Tema) was originally intended to be a temporary settlement for the non-native residents who were displaced in the development of Tema. Tema was purposefully designed as an industrial and port city through land acquisition (166 square km) from the chiefs and people of Nungua in 1952. Pieces of timber and corrugated roofing sheets from demolished structure in the Tema site were provided to commence the temporary settlement, and, as such, planning for its future development was not given the necessary consideration. Ashaiman's proximity to Tema and the lack of building codes led to cheaper rental accommodation. Its population was 185 in 1948 and rose to 2,624 in 1960. By that time, permanent houses were preferred and constructed. The Tema Development Corporation set up an office at Ashaiman in 1966 to enforce building regulations but could not bring the situation under control. The population of Ashaiman increased to 22,000 in 1970, 50,000 in 1984, and 75,000 in 1996. By the year 2020 it had reached a population of more than 300,000.[31]

Nima, another area considered as a slum, was initially used as pastureland for cattle by the Futa family in the 1930s. Even though the Nima lands are owned by the Nii Odoi Kwao family, they did not have outright control. In the decades following the expansion of Accra, at the outset of World War II, it became a residential location for many.[32] Urban planning schemes were not prepared for Nima because it was not under the jurisdiction of the Accra Local government.

City planners cannot have the necessary impact without input from the community for whose benefit a plan is developed. Again, planning is about change. It involves preventing the undesirable and encouraging the appropriate. It is not always about law enforcement, but incentives and financial support for city inhabitants equally play a role. Any activity or program that will ensure change is a good planning tool. Solving the issue of slums should be tailored to getting decent and alternative accommodation for the slum dwellers. Addressing tenancy issues, providing temporary accommodation, tax incentives, zoning ordinances, density bonuses, etc.,[33] are some of the ways to practically improve the life of the slum dweller.

The "Site and Services" program which involved subdividing large tracts of land into small land plots, and then installing the necessary infrastructure such as water, sewerage, and roads, remains viable. This was a popular housing planning methodology advocated by the World Bank, United Nations, and other International Aid Agencies. In a typical sites and services program, a Housing Authority will provide the serviced land, while the building of a house on the site is left to the individual developer.[34] It has more success rates when the areas selected for development are close to jobs and also when the projects are not heavily subsidized by the public sector.[35]

Old Fadama- Slum Upgrading or Slum Clearance?

Located on the outskirts of Accra, along the Odaw River and Korle Lagoon, Old Fadama is home to more than 80,000 people. Regarded as the slum capital of Ghana, the settlement is characterized by dilapidated housing, overcrowding, poverty, and social vices. The households in Old Fadama lack access to sanitation, water, secure tenure, and sufficient living area. Meeting the most essential elements of human sustenance (health, shelter, jobs, and education) is a struggle for many residents of Old Fadama. To find a sustainable solution to the slum menace at Old Fadama, the government of Ghana must, as a matter of urgency, decide whether to upgrade the slum or clear it completely (evict the residents with adequate compensation) and undertake high density commercial and residential development.

Is slum upgrading the way to go? Slum upgrading is an option which has succeeded in many places. The retention of a substantial percentage of the slum population is key to any slum improvement project. It involves the progressive improvement of the physical, social, and economic environment of a settlement for the benefit of existing residents, with minimal disturbance or displacement. Improving the water supply, drainage, sanitation, roads, footpaths, and refuse disposal are the foundation for a successful slum upgrading project. Displacement is minimal.[36] A successful slum upgrading project at Old Fadama must begin with addressing security of tenure of residents. Without the security of tenure, many slum dwellers would not wish to invest in their dwellings. Most parts of the settlement fall within environmentally sensitive areas, and as such, are not conducive for horizontal development of housing. Cluster development in the form of multi-family mid-rise apartments and row houses would have to be employed to

Old Fadama, Accra

ensure that only the most favorable portions of the land are used for housing. Slum dwellers must be educated and supported with programs that will make them economically independent and plan adequately for the future.[37] Identification of slum dwellers is also key. Knowing the trends and monitoring changes over time is necessary. More professional involvement of architects, planners, urban designers, and engineers is required. Volunteers of professionals can help educate slum dwellers on basic construction skills.

Creating vehicular access to Old Fadama will aid in efficient monitoring of activities within the settlement. The ad hoc construction of kiosks and how haphazardly they are situated make vehicular access to Old Fadama difficult. Emergency services cannot maneuver through the slum in cases of fire outbreak or riot. Providing alleys and streets, and spatially coordinating the dwellings would help improve security and solve the issues of insecurity and crime. Presently, improvements are not made to their dwellings because of the constant threat of demolition and eviction. When given assurances from the government, many slum dwellers would not hesitate to improve their built structures. The government's support for building vertically in slum areas would make it easier for the provision of parks, playgrounds, and enough green spaces. These are all fundamental to the healthy growth of children and the wellbeing of community members. Most importantly, the collection of data, tracking of trends, and undertaking of frequent studies at Old Fadama would become imperative. Population changes are important to track, including deaths, births, and other statistics, to properly measure what improvements should be made with the programs and policies that would be rolled out. Feedback from residents regarding effectiveness of interventions is crucial. If the rich and wealthy corporations and individuals can channel some of their resources to slum upgrading, many lives would be transformed.

Will ecological sanctity lead the government to pursue slum clearance? Due to the severity of the inhumane living conditions at Old Fadama, successive governments have attempted slum clearance in the past with minimal success. The inability of successive governments to find alternative locations that appeal to the residents suggests that a well-thought-out plan must be in place before such an approach is used. Many slum dwellers would welcome affordable housing in fairly decent neighborhoods. Not all residents of Old Fadama live in abject poverty. Residents of the settlement continue to stay in the slum due to lack of affordable housing in Accra. The government has to create incentives to lure residents to other locations. The provision of these new housing projects should be accompanied with a commercial zone or a business district so that residents can continue to trade and find employment opportunities to ensure its effectiveness. For instance, a modern market can be built in the new location as part of the resettlement plan.

A successful slum clearance will allow for the rehabilitation of the Korle Lagoon and lay the foundation for urban revitalization of the area, with large-scale commercial and residential development with waterfront amenities. Not only will such development be economically viable, but it will greatly improve the tourism potential of the capital city. For now, clearing of slum will bring added problems since homelessness will be unbearable and compounded by the ongoing effects of COVID-19.

Irrespective of the option the government chooses, it has to be done in a timely manner and the more time that lapses, the more complex the situation becomes. People Dialogue on Human Settlement together with Slum Dwellers International have been doing remarkable work at Old Fadama, but the government's active involvement and strong collaboration with these organizations would help find a permanent solution to slums. Visionary leaders are needed to implement policies that will bring long term solutions. It would be difficult to embark on slum transformation or clearance without political will. Systematic social mediation would be needed in finding lasting solutions to the issues surrounding this settlement. Most slum dwellers work in the informal sector—economic activities that are not registered for the purposes of taxes or for social security.[38] On-the-job training and apprenticeships are good measures to elevate the skill levels of slum dwellers.[39] Reducing fertility rates through family planning programs is important in slum communities. The number of children a woman will have in her lifetime directly impacts her employment trajectory and her ability to develop her talents. Birth rates drop only when education spreads and people come to understand that too many children are an economic liability if not properly planned. Educated women generally put contraceptives to good use.[40]

Learning from Curitiba

Curitiba, a Brazilian city of more than two million people is often cited as a good example of the success of planning. Useful elements are available on how Curitiba can help in the transformation of some of the slums and squatter settlements in the major cities of Ghana. The transformation of Curitiba into a green/ecological city was a result of the leadership of the architect Jaime Lerner, mayor of the city for three terms starting 1969.[41] He established the transit system in early 1970s and oversaw the planning process.

In 1943, the French urbanist Alfred Agache developed a masterplan to guide Curitiba's development. With a population of 470,000 and a population growth of 5% in the early 1960s, the municipality decided that a new plan was needed. An ideas competition was organized for proposals on the future city, and in 1965 a new masterplan was proposed by Jorge Wilheim that was the winning scheme. The Institute for Research and Urban Planning (IPPUC) was formed in 1966 to implement the masterplan. Zoning laws were enacted to increase the density in areas of the city linked to transportation. The powerful in society rallied around masterplan and the media played the role of disseminating program schemes. The benefits reached all the way to lower income groups.[42]

In 1969, planners in Curitiba decided to focus on mass transit system rather than on cars. Seventy-two percent of the population depend on buses for movement throughout the city. Their zoning laws allow for only high-rise apartments near the major bus routes. The first two floors of apartments were designated as stores. More than 145 kilometers of bike lanes have been built throughout the city and cars are banned in certain areas of the Central Business District. A network of bike lanes, pedestrian walkways, bus terminals, and parks have been implemented instead.[43] The city turned flood prone areas along its rivers into a series of parks and bike lanes. Squatter settlement also benefit from water, sewage, and bus services. Clean running water is a top priority for the local government because it aids in reducing the spread of infectious diseases.

Planting of trees are encouraged with volunteers planting in excess of 1.5 million trees. Permits are required before any tree can be cut and two trees must be planted for each tree cut down. Sixty percent of the metal, glass, plastic, and 70% of paper collected from households are recycled and sold to major industries who then apply strict pollution standards in its use.

Education is also a key element in Curitiba's success. Ninety-five percent of its citizens are literate with 83% having a high school education. Ecology is taught to all school children. Old buses are used as mobile classrooms to train the poor on the basic skills needed for jobs. Other buses are retrofitted and used as health clinics, soup kitchens, and daycare centers. One of the most interesting aspects of the city planning is that it assists the poor. Poor families are given plots of land, building materials, two tree seedlings to plant, and two hour-long consultations with an architect.[44] Cities in Ghana have a lot to learn from Curitiba in our attempt to deal with the spatial chaos and in the design of future cities. Transforming slums is possible with the political will of the central government and the commitment of slum dwellers.

CHAPTER 7
ZONING AND MASTER PLANNING

The haphazard infrastructure development in Ghana's major cities calls into question the effectiveness of planning institutions and law enforcement. Property developers have embarked on scattered projects that have no overall impact on the visual form of cities because they are disconnected. These projects have become eyesores in cities like Accra and Kumasi and have deviated from the architectural landscapes of neighborhoods within the cities. This situation is more worrisome because of the abundance of talented architects, engineers, and planners in the country who are not being used or using their talents to build upon and champion the numerous planning-related laws that can right these wrongs.

The heavy development pressure in the major cities like Accra and Kumasi makes Ghana's climate resilience fight difficult and at times questionable. The government's policies are not in alignment with the rate of development pressure experienced in these cities, and, more importantly, public health, safety, and welfare of community

Pokuase

members are not the guiding principles for these developments: gas stations are built in non-conforming zones, extensions are made to existing residential facilities without permit, and the proliferation of churches in residential zones have become common in most neighborhoods in major cities. Most of the issues faced in these cities could have been avoided or minimized had there been masterplans and zoning ordinances to guide development after independence. Planning helps to check suburban sprawl and ensures new buildings or developments are undertaken in context of existing properties bordering the new development. Building regulations address safety, use, and environmental impact concerns. Planning laws regulate the appearance, siting, and zoning of the built environment.[1] The rapid rate of development in the urban areas requires dedication and a lot of discipline on the part of developers, landowners, and the local authorities.

There are three types of assemblies which make up the local government system in Ghana: Metropolitan Assembly (for a city or large town with a population over 250,000), Municipal Assembly (a single town's local government area with a population of over 95,000), and a District Assembly (a local government area comprising a district capital and other small centers and rural area with a population of over 75,000). The Municipal Assembly must consist of a single compact development.[2] Every Metropolitan, Municipal, and District Assembly should have a team of experienced planners, architects, and engineers.

In 2008, for instance, only 64 out of the 170 MMDAs had professional planners. It is non-negotiable that all MMDAs should have licensed spatial planners who can readily interpret the zoning requirements to developers and the general public. This is done to ensure that developers have a thorough understanding of maximum coverage of land, maximum height, and the bulk of building and density standards, as well as contextual design and an understanding of the goals for structure and form in the district—even before development permits are sought. Special exceptions should be granted sparingly and with due diligence to inure to the benefits of the districts. The guiding principle should be that any design plans presented to the District Assembly for permit should be guided by a design philosophy that will contribute positively to the district, and not be a disfigurement to the architectural character of any community in the district. The training of more spatial planners and urban designers in our tertiary institutions is a matter of urgency.

After Ghana's independence in 1957, the Institute for Community Planning was set up to train local planning assistants who will work on planning schemes primarily in the rural areas. This was to enable the extension of planning activities. A team was also set up for the preparation of a National Physical Development Plan, within which all detail schemes will in the future be planned. Model building regulations were published in 1960 and distributed to all municipal and urban councils with strong recommendation for their adoption.[3] These measures were not followed by successive governments.

Plan Making and Zoning in Principle

A plan is an adopted statement of policy in the form of texts, maps, and graphics used to guide public and private actions that affect the future. A plan provides decision makers with information they need to make informed decisions affecting the long-range social, economic, and physical growth of a community. There are different kinds of plans that guide the development of cities. They include comprehensive plans, urban design plans, a transportation plan, a conservation plan, etc. The Plan's core is the statement of authority to prepare and adopt a plan. It includes: (i) background data, including area history, existing conditions and trends, and data projections; (ii) documentation of stakeholder interest and stakeholder involvement process; (iii) a vision statement or statement of goals and objectives for future conditions; (iv) an evaluation of plan and design alternatives; and (v) a program of implementation.

The planning process is carried out to ensure that solutions are found to the problems of a community. The process begins with identifying issues and options, then the goals, objectives, and priorities are stated clearly. A goal is a statement that describes, usually in general terms, a desired future condition, and an objective is a statement that describes a specific condition to be attained within a stated period of time. After the goals and objectives, data is collected and interpreted. The preparation of the plan can then begin. Programs are drafted for the implementation of the plan. The impacts of the plan and implementation programs are evaluated before the plan is reviewed and adopted. The implementation programs are also reviewed and adopted before they are administered. In the plan preparation process, MMDAs must work with a wide range of stakeholders to ensure its success. Residents, landowners, renters, neighborhood business owners, environmental groups, religious organizations, civic groups, neighborhood associations, members of parliament, etc., all have roles to play as stakeholders.

A comprehensive plan is a document (adopted official statement of a local government) outlining the vision of a community for its desired future development (usually 15–20 years) and conservation. It serves as a guide for the zoning ordinance. Through the comprehensive plan, the present conditions of different areas of a community are identified. An assessment is carried out on the population growth and development trends, followed by an analysis of the relationship between housing, transportation, community facilities, and the local economy. Based on the extensive study, the plan designates areas to be preserved, areas for future development, and areas where improvement is required.[4] The elements of a comprehensive plan may include historic preservation, parks, recreation and open spaces, farmland preservation, natural hazard responses, economic development, urban design, housing, and transportation.

Urban Design Plan: Urban design plans give three-dimensional physical form to policies enumerated by a comprehensive plan. Public spaces and the buildings that define them are the ingredients that create the public realm. Urban design plans contain a section on design guidelines. They address issues related to placement, sun, shadow, wind, massing, height, building setbacks, architectural style, parking, streetscapes, signage, materials, and sustainable design. Urban design plans require interdisciplinary collaboration among urban designers, architects, landscape architects, planners, civil and environmental engineers, and market analysts.

Zoning Regulations: Zoning is a tool used by local city governments and planning authorities to prescribe the acceptable use and form of development of land within a community. It is the most direct tool for guiding private development toward fulfilling the objectives of the comprehensive plan.[5] Zoning typically regulates three aspects of built form: function, shape, and bulk. Zoning laws divide areas under a local government jurisdiction into sub-areas or districts and determine the uses it can be put to. Zoning emerged in the nineteenth century, with the Germans being the first to employ this technique.[6] Zones are defined as an area whose boundaries can be accurately geo-referenced within 20 meters. For instance, the

1916 New York City Zoning Code was designed to regulate height and bulk of skyscrapers. The regulation stemmed from a concern of buildings overshadowing others by casting dark shadows over streets and older buildings. The principle of floor area ratio was applied to plot size and frontage in an effort to contain threats to property values.[7]

To create a zoning ordinance, a local government authority will divide its jurisdiction into zones/districts. It spells out allowable uses for each zone such as agriculture, industry, commercial, and residential use. For each district or zone, the zoning ordinance regulates (i) the type of land uses allowed; (ii) intensity and density of development; (iii) height, bulk, and placement of construction; (iv) amount and design of parking; and (v) a number of other aspects of land use and development activity.

The use standards of a zoning ordinance identify the land uses and the restrictions or limitations specific to each permitted use for each zoning district. Uses are typically classified according to several criteria: (i) permitted "by right uses"; (ii) permitted conditional or special uses; (iii) permitted accessory uses; and (iv) prohibited uses. Intensity and density standards cover maximum density, minimum lot size, and the maximum floor area (FAR). Dimensional standards address the bulk and scale of development. For each zoning district they typically include one or more of the following: (i) maximum building height; (ii) minimum yard depth or minimum building setback; (iii) maximum front and side setbacks; (iv) maximum building coverage; (v) maximum impervious surface; and (vi) maximum building size or building envelope standards.[8]

Seeking planning and development approval is compulsory because of the comprehensive plan and zoning ordinances. Applying for a planning permission involves presenting your scheme design, an ordnance survey drawing showing the site location plan, a filled-out application form as prescribed by the local government and the Land Use and Spatial Planning Authority (LUSPA). In other jurisdictions, a written statement in the form of a letter or report is attached to the filled-out application. The design philosophy is briefly explained in the statement. The impact of a developer's building on the adjoining buildings, if any, or any contributions the building will make in the locality are assessed.[9] The right of government to regulate personal conduct of individuals and property owners in their use of land, as a way of protecting the public health, safety, and welfare of community members is known as police power. Through laws and ordinances, the government can preserve public order and tranquility and promote the public health, safety, morals, and general welfare. In America, the police powers are vested in states and they in turn grant it to local governments through charters and enabling statutes. In Ghana, it is not expressly stated but is achieved through a panoply of laws.

In terms of land use administration, at the county level there is a Board of Supervisors, at city level there is a City Council, and at the town level there is a Town Council. The local governing body is the local legislature, only the courts can overturn a legislative decision. In addition to the local governing body, each locality has a planning commission. The planning commission is responsible for the development of the comprehensive plan and proposed plan amendments. They also review zoning ordinances and sometimes review site plans and subdivision plans. The Board of Zoning Appeals (BZA) is responsible for hearing appeals from orders, requirements, decisions, and determinations made by the zoning administrator or other local government staff. In some localities, the BZA is authorized by the governing body to issue special permits or special exceptions under the zoning ordinance. The zoning administrator interprets and enforces the zoning ordinance. The planning staff is responsible for providing advice and technical assistance to the planning commission, the local governing body, and the BZA. They review all landowner applications for comprehensive plan or zoning ordinance amendments and also review subdivision and site plans to ensure that they comply with local regulations.

Public participation is an essential part of land use administration. Planning decisions fall into two general categories: legislative and administrative. Opportunities for public participation are substantially greater for legislative decisions than they are for administrative decisions. Legislative decisions include the adoption and amendment of ordinances, the adoption and amendment of the comprehensive plan, and the issuance of special exceptions. Due process must be applied in land use administration. Procedural due process requires that a person be given notice of a government action that will affect their property before the action takes place. It also requires that the property owner be given an opportunity to be heard before it acts and that a duly constituted elected body approves the action. Substantive due process examines the effects of a regulation on the property owner (versus fairness of the process of enacting the regulation). It requires first that there be a legitimate public purpose behind a regulation and second, that there be a substantial relationship between the regulation and the purpose.

Zoning in Ghana

The decentralized national development planning system comprises the district development planning authorities at the district level, regional coordinating council at the regional level, and sector agencies, ministries, and the National Development Planning Commission at the national level. Ghana operates a three-tier planning system. The spatial planning framework, the structural plan, and the local plan. The spatial development framework is for the national level, regional level, sub-regional level, and district level. The structure of the plan is a long term (10–15-year) statutory framework used to guide the development or redevelopment of land. It is used to define the future development and land-use patterns, the layout of transportation routes, conservation, and protected areas and other key features for managing the direction of development.[10]

The structure plan lays out the different zones and outline the types of development that will be detailed at the plot level in a local plan. A range of color codes are used in the structure plan

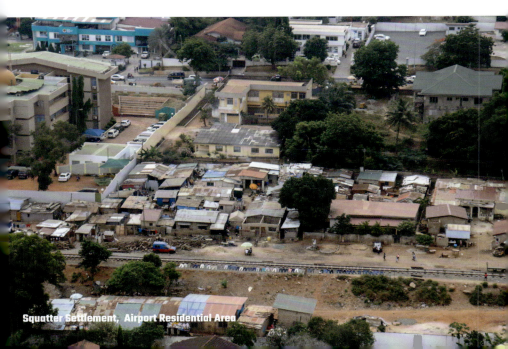

Squatter Settlement, Airport Residential Area

to depict the different zones/districts. A report and a zoning plan make up the structure plan. A financial plan will also be prepared for the implementation of the structure plan to consider the capital, operations, and management costs as well as sources of funding. A local plan includes the spatial arrangement for the development of prescribed areas and contain provisions for orderly, coordinated, efficient, and environmentally sound development and proper use of land in the district. The local plan (prepared for a five-year period) specifies the intended use of all parcels of land within the plan area. It details the use standards for specific development. Use standards are classifications based on land uses which are permitted, land uses that are prohibited, and land uses that come with additional conditions.

The planning system has faced numerous challenges. Both urban and rural cities do not show any significant traces of effective zoning. In 2011, as part of the Constitution Review Commission (CRC), the planning system in Ghana was assessed. Among the findings was that the success of a National Development Plan was dependent on the citizens owning and cherishing it. There must therefore be full participation of citizens through a bottom up and decentralized approach. The CRC recommended broad consultation with a wide range of stakeholders and grassroots included, as well as a requirement of a two-thirds majority approval in parliament before a plan becomes operational through a constitutional amendment.

It was recommended that the NDPC should only develop the plan and facilitate, monitor, and evaluate its implementation while the Ministries, Departments, and Agencies (MDAs) and MMDAs be primarily responsible for implementing the national development plan. To ensure continuity, the president of Ghana has to report to the parliament of Ghana once a year and update parliament on all steps taken to ensure the implementation of the national development plan.

Land Ownership in Ghana

Land ownership in Ghana falls under customary (80%) or public ownership (20%). Public land is made up of state land and vested land. Customary land is made up of stool, skin, clan, family, and individual land. Eighteen percent of the public land was compulsorily acquired. The institutions involved in land administration are the Public and Vested Land Management Division, Lands Commission,

Land Valuation Board, Customary Land Secretariat, Office of the Administrator of Stool Lands, and the Survey and Mapping Division. There are five types of land interest rights in Ghana: (i) allodial interest: held by stools, skins, *tendamba*, sub-stools, or clans or families depending on the customary law prevailing in the area; (ii) customary freehold: right of usufruct to which members of land-owning communities are entitled in the customary law of that community; (iii) common law freehold: arising out of an express freehold grant by the allodial title owner through outright sale or gift; (iv) lease hold interest: including subleases granted to a person to occupy and use land for a specified period, subject to certain covenants and the payment of an agreed rent; and (v) customary tenancies: which are usually contractual arrangements to occupy land for a period in exchange for either a specific portion of produce to the landlord at harvest time or for an agreed rent.[11]

Article 267 (3) of the 1992 constitution of Ghana provides that there shall be no disposition or development of any stool land unless the Regional Lands Commission of the region in which the land is situated has certified that the disposition or development is consistent with the development plan drawn up or approved by the planning authority for the area concerned. This provision seems to have been ignored in the development process in many cities in Ghana. Traditional leaders have not worked well with land administration institutions to ensure that the rights of purchasers of land are protected. Land disputes and issues have plagued Ghana for many centuries. Many scholars have argued that the system of ownership of land in Ghana has halted the needed development. It is difficult to predict what the state of affairs in Ghana would have been if the majority of land in Ghana belonged to the state. Sale of a piece of land to multiple people and development of land in disregard of structure and local plans by both developers, traditional leaders, and the government has led to many disputes. Chiefs hold sway in land issues in Ghana but some of their decisions have not been in the best interest of their people. It is admirable how, through the bravery of the chiefs and the local people, the colonial powers were unable to take over their lands. Despite the resistance of the chiefs, Ghana's lands have been poorly managed. Under the Native Jurisdiction Ordinance (NJO) of 1878, the destoolment of chiefs was common because of the granting of land concessions to European concessionaires and farmers from other tribes. Decisions were not taken with the support of their councils, families were deprived of their lands, and misappropriation of monetary compensations received prevailed.[12] The tendency for some chiefs to assume more powers of control over land than what the general community and council approve of was common then and now.

The amendment of the NJO in 1927 to the Native Administration Ordinance (NAO) were key events in 1894 and 1897. It was the intention of the colonial administration in 1894 to prevent the largescale offering of land to mining and timber companies operating in the country. The measure taken was to propose an ordinance vesting all waste land (unused, unoccupied, or undeveloped land) in the crown. This step generated widespread opposition from locals who maintained that it was still the property of the stool or tribe. The chief, as a trustee of the tribal land supported by his council, are allowed to or within their right to make grants and settle all disputes accruing from boundary disputes between different families.[13] Still desirous of vesting all undeveloped tribal lands in the crown, in 1897 a second attempt was made with the Lands Bill, which was an ordinance to regulate the administration of public land and define the parameters of a concession. The opposition to the move was such that the colonial government had to refer the Lands Bill to the secretary of state. Those opposed, launched an appeal to the secretary of state. A Concession Ordinance was passed in 1900 enabling the supreme court of the colony to review all proposed concessions and modify the term it considered unreasonable.

Ethical Land Use

In many countries, the local government imposes conditions on development, which require developers to restore damaged environmental features because of their development. So, felling of trees, mining, etc., have to be done in a careful way. The ecological integrity of the planet is under threat from unguided land use actions like galamsey, water pollution, and air pollution. Urbanization and population growth are making this situation even worse. The modification of climate through the loss of the natural environment has left cities vulnerable to climatic and environmental disaster.[14] Wetlands are known to control flooding, serve as biological spawning grounds for commercially important fish, and are used for recreational uses. Losing the wetlands for any form of development eliminates these natural benefits and can be difficult and costly to replicate. Land use practices that encourage mixed use, walkable neighborhoods will help in protecting the natural environment. Areas under threat/high hazard must be purchased by the government so that enforcing their protection is easier because they cease to be viable land for private developers. Protecting the vegetative cover will reduce the rate of endangered plant and animal species, and their loss will negatively affect tourism, and medical and scientific research.[15]

Mortgage Financing

A mortgage (charge): *the name for the charge over land, that is the security for the loan granted by a bank to the purchaser of the land, rather than the name for the loan itself.* It is not the bank that grants the mortgage, but rather the purchaser in return for a loan. The purchaser does not own the land at the time he/she arranges to borrow the money, but he/she agrees to grant a mortgage as soon as he/she becomes the owner.[16] The borrower who grants the mortgage to the bank is a mortgagor. The lender, who in return for receiving the mortgage lends the money, is a mortgagee. Mortgage financing involves providing loans to potential home buyers so that they can borrow to support their purchases. There are four main loan categories: (i) a home purchase mortgage: used for purchasing new houses. The borrower is normally expected to make a minimum 20–25% down payment of the value of the property. The loan term is usually for 15 years and the interest rates are always liable to change; (ii) a home improvement mortgage: intended for renovation of already acquired property; (iii) a home completion mortgage: used to complete a house under construction; and (iv) a home equity mortgage: used for realizing equity locked up in a property.[17]

All property that is not real property, including leasehold land, and often used as the opposite to "fixture" is called chattel. Any provision in a mortgage deed that restricts the mortgagor's equity of redemption is called clogs and fetters. Any real property having a physical form is called corporeal hereditament. The owner of the land that benefits from an easement is called a dominant owner. Land that has the benefit of the easement is the dominant tenement. The value, that is, the difference between the monetary worth of a property and the amount of outstanding mortgage debt is the equity. A lease that grants an interest in land on terms that correspond to those of a legal lease but without completion of the legal formalities is an equitable lease. The bundle of rights given by law to the mortgagor, which includes the equitable right of redemption, is the equity of redemption. The right of the mortgagor to repay all of the capital, interest, and costs involved in their mortgage arrangement at any time, and thereby wholly own their property, is equitable right of redemption. A mortgage under which the mortgagee does not acquire a legal interest in the land is equitable mortgage.

The length of time for granting land to a tenant under the system of tenure is estate. A feudal system is a political, economic, and social system under which only the monarch is able to own land outright. Any object attached to the land in such a way and for such reason that it becomes part of the land is called a fixture. Foreclosure is a remedy under which the court orders a date by which the mortgagor must pay his/her debt, or on which his/her property will be lost to the mortgagee. Gazumping is the process of a third party offering, or the vendor accepting a higher offer on a property on which a sale price has already been agreed, but for which agreement, no binding contract is yet in place. Gazundering is the process of a purchaser demanding a lower price on a property after a sale price has already been agreed, but for which no binding contract has being signed. "Interest only mortgage" is a type of mortgage arrangement under which the mortgagor repays only interest each month, with capital to be repaid in full at the end of the mortgage term. A legal lease is a lease that creates an estate in land for a term of years absolute and with certain formalities. A legal mortgage is a mortgage that is created by legal charge (in registered land) and completed by means of certain formalities. Legal charge is a legal interest in land that acts to secure the payment of money.

Negative equity is a negative value that arises when the monetary worth of a property is less than the amount of outstanding mortgage debt. Personal Property is property that does not comprise freehold land. Real property (or realty) refers to freehold land. Repayment mortgage is a type of mortgage arrangement under which the mortgagor repays both interest and capital each month. The owner of the land that bears the burden of an easement is the servient owner. The land that bears the burden of the easement is the servient tenement. Solus tie is a type of agreement that binds the mortgagor into buying products only from the mortgagee. The adding of a further advance of money under an existing mortgage agreement, subject to certain conditions is called tacking. The ownership of two plots of land by the same (legal) person is called unity of seisin.[18] Usufruct is the legal right to use and derive profit from property belonging to someone else provided that the property itself is not injured in anyway. A cadastral map shows or records property boundaries, subdivision lines, buildings, and related details.

Protecting the City's Image

A city is composed of component districts (industrial areas, university campuses, residential areas, etc.). The termination of a district is its edge. A seam is formed when two districts are joined. The major and minor routes of circulation (streets, canals, railroads, walkways) that people use to move about are the pathways. Landmarks are the prominent or distinct visual features (buildings, signs, stores, and mountains) of a city. As an important element of the urban form, they help people to identify an area and also orient themselves in the city.[19] A node or core is a distinct center of activity. They are the strategic spots or points in a city into which an observer can enter. It is technically a type of landmark but unique by virtue of its active function.[20] The raw material of the environmental image at the city scale are the districts, pathways, nodes, and landmarks. To heighten the imageability of the urban environment is to facilitate its visual identification and structuring through the raw materials. People of diverse class and character build and inhabit a city. The multiplicity of builders enhances a constant modification of the city. The total control of its growth and form is thus impossible. General outlines can guide its growth but not in minute details.

    A stratified and gigantic order will therefore not be exhibited but city designers must make provisions for paths, edges, landmarks, nodes, and districts to enhance the form. Different patterns may

Opportunities for Infill Development

emerge such as linear, ring, star branch, etc. The controls instituted to achieve visual form at the city scale may include zoning ordinances, positive design of all governmental projects, persuasive influence over private developments, and massive incentives for foreign investment in infrastructure. Such measures are unfortunately not being attempted in Ghana. The urban fabric seems not to be of concern to political leaders. The neglect of form and the preference for a piecemeal approach to city development has left the city in disarray.[21] A lot has to be done to build the right image for Ghanaian cities and establish the right mechanism to protect its image.

Planning Terminologies

If a government takes, expropriates, acquires, or seizes property without compensation it is referred to as a taking. Taking also refers to any government action that denies economically viable use of property. Regulatory taking refers to land for which the use has been so heavily regulated that it effectively becomes a form of eminent domain. Vested property right is a right that has been legally established and cannot be resolved by subsequent conditions or changes in law without due process of law. Vested rights statutes may also provide that developers are not protected against certain regulations intended to address substantial public safety concerns. The zoning of property generally does not confer a vested right protection against its subsequent rezoning. Form based zoning establishes zones of building type based on pedestrian accessibility and the scale and character of the surrounding development, but largely allows building owners to determine how the buildings will be used. Incentive zoning is used to overcome strict site regulations of height and/or bulk; it provides a developer with flexibility and encourages certain land uses and project features. Overlay zoning/floating zoning provides for the possibility of super-imposing a certain additional requirement upon a basic use zoning district without disturbing the requirement of the basic use district. Sliding scale zoning reduces the allowable dwelling units as land parcels get bigger. It works on the principle that the larger the parcel of land, the greater the agricultural resource it represents, and therefore, the potential for development to be limited. To avoid imposing "undue hardship" on a landowner, a site-specific exception may be made to the provisions of a zoning ordinance called a variance. Up zoning refers to changing the zoning of a tract or parcel of land from a lesser to a greater intensity of usage. Down zoning is an amendment to a zoning ordinance that changes the zoning and reduces the zoning potential of the land. Land banking is where a local government purchases and reserves land for future development.

Conservation easement is a voluntary agreement between a landowner and an easement holder restricting development on a parcel of land. The easement holder may be a public agency, a non-governmental agency (NGO), or conservation entity. Easement is when a property owner grants to the public the use of his/her land for specific purposes (such as drainage ways, utility lines, roadways, etc.), and is created when a third party enjoys and has engaged a right over a property for a number of years. An area may be designated as an enterprise zone where planning controls are kept at a minimum and attractive financial incentives are offered to prospective developers and occupants. When the government takes or damages property without first paying just compensation or filing a lawsuit to acquire the property, an inverse condemnation has occurred. The local government can stop reviewing new building permits for a specific period, called a moratorium, allowing them time to change policies in times of heavy development pressure.

Nuisance refers to the use of property by a property holder in a manner that seriously interferes with another property holder's use or enjoyment, and such use may be injurious to the community at large. Exactions are conditions set by a local government that require the landowner to convey a property interest, which is typically negotiated between the landowner and the local government during the permitting process for development.[22] It is sometimes a contribution or payment required as an authorized precondition for receiving a development permit. In some situations, before the zoning ordinance comes into effect, a landowner is allowed to recoup the value of a non-conforming use within a particular period, known as amortization. Planning that is done to deal with the expected impact of climate change is called anticipatory planning. In some situations, people are encouraged to sell their property by creating the impression that a neighborhood is changing for the worse (usually racial makeup), which is known as block busting. The clear, direct, and substantial relationship between a particular development and the public improvement needs generated by the development is known as a rational nexus. A map, drawn to scale, showing the divisions of a piece of land is a subdivision plats/cadastral map.

Subdivision ordinances are regulations that govern the subdivision of large tracts of land into smaller parcels for the purpose of transfer of ownership, building, and development purposes. They regulate how large tracts of land are subdivided into individually saleable lots. Cluster development is applied to large tracts of land with different site characteristics and is when plot sizes are reduced in favor of common open space areas. This allows for utilization of the best building sites while preserving environmentally sensitive areas. Under planned unit development (PUD), zoning and subdivision controls are merged allowing developers to undertake the planning and development of a large area as a single entity. PUD gives developers the flexibility to mix land uses, housing types, and densities. The development can be phased over a number of years.

Local governments can make use of the zoning ordinance to designate areas in a community where development should be discouraged. Transfer of development credit allows the property owners within these development restricted areas (called sending areas) to give up development credits and sell them to areas where development is being encouraged (called the receiving areas) by the local government. The purchaser can use the credit to exceed development densities, floor areas, or building heights in the receiving area. Receiving area landowners receive financial compensation.[23] The development credit is monetized by the level of development the base zoning ordinance would allow.

CHAPTER 8
STREET LAYOUT AND CITY PLANNING

Every human settlement largely reflects the beliefs, social life, and the need of all its inhabitants. The early village sometimes occupied an acre or two and was inhabited by fewer than a dozen families. The village practiced long term planning and patient application to common task.[1] Leon Battista Alberti is of the view that the principal ornament to any city lies in the siting, layout, composition, and arrangement of its roads, squares, and individual works; each must be properly planned and distributed according to use, importance, and convenience. Without order there can be nothing commodious, graceful, or noble. This assertion, I believe, is something many city planners wholeheartedly agree with. Linear based urban planning schemes present problems that are more complex, especially in the organization of demographic growth.[2] In some countries, the layout of streets and arrangement of buildings was determined by the ancient art of geomancy. In the great and noble city called Cambulac, "The City of the Emperor," the great Khan was informed

Accra Mall, Accra

by his astrologers that the proposed city would prove rebellious and raise great disorder against his imperial authority, so he had the new city built beside the old one with only a river between them and forced the people of the old city to be removed to the new town he founded.[3] While geomancy is not as commonly practiced now, there are many considerations that factor into the building of cities in our world now.

Grid Street System

The simple geometric plan was the foundation for city building under the pharaohs because it allowed for rapid building. The level land was a factor in the planning choice for settlements. It was rigorous and systematic. Organic plans, on the other hand, were achieved through decision making of many generations based on their developmental needs. This led to the subtle and complex richness of form.[4] It was spontaneous and irregular. The organic and the geometric forms were thus two basic city forms to emerge early in Western civilization. Geography, climate, and land apportionment shaped both forms, but while geometric cities were planned, functional, and rational, the organic cities arose by chance and accretion and grew randomly. Rome, for instance, was built with both organic origins and gridded streets. The city had to

Street Layout should enhance walkability

be rebuilt at least six times and experienced successive periods of growth and decay.[5] The grid originated to support military efficiency and taxation in Greek and Roman settlement. The Romans created many new towns based on the standard castrum plan with two main thoroughfares crossing each other at right angles, a forum in the center, and public buildings (theater, thermae) arranged within the logical grid plan.[6] Marcus Vitrivius Pollio suggested that towns should be centrally planned for defense. Leon Battista Alberti and Antonio di Pietro Averlino (Filarete) proposed formal, geometrical, polygonal town plans surrounded by massive fortification to resist the might of modern artillery. For the Greeks, city planning involved rationality and order but was done in a unique, pragmatic arrangement suited to topographical, historical, and practical specifications.[7] The use of the grid became very popular in the planning of cities. Greek city planning was based on the idea that the form of cities, the shape of the street and spaces, reflected the people who inhabited them. The Hippodamian Scheme, originated by Hippodamus, forms the basis by which the grid is utilized. The city was cut by several main streets crossing at right angles. The resulting rectangles were subdivided into a relatively uniform grid of *insulae* (blocks), the rectangular blocks were then further subdivided into house plots. Public buildings were set within the system without interfering with traffic. The scheme was adapted to the terrain. The use of the Hippodamian Scheme by many American cities was owed largely to a desire to facilitate efficient land distribution and development in a society that believed strongly in the moral benefit of owning real estate.[8] The abundance of land has led to the proliferation of low-density development and the wealth of American natural resources has equally fostered the widespread use of high-quality building materials. Their architectural landscape is therefore unique in many ways.[9]

In America, the typical urban grid was formed by subdividing 40 square acres. Under the Land Ordinance Survey of 1795, 40 square acres was typically divided into 5-acre rectangles called "blocks," each block roughly 200m by 100m (660ft by 330ft). Both George Washington and Thomas Jefferson believed that grid geometry represented the democratic principles upon which America was founded. This belief reflected the fundamental role property played in the American idea of democracy. The founding fathers, who were all men of property, saw real estate as a fundamental right of each citizen. They established ownership as a precondition to voting in the early nation, probably in part because having land seemed likely to assure economic freedom in an agrarian economy. Such freedom remained unattainable in Europe, where only a privileged few owned land. When Congress passed the legislation for disbursing land, it altered Jefferson's original plan by creating "townships of six miles [10 kilometers] square subdivided into thirty-six sections of one square mile each [1.6 km].[10] The city plan for Philadelphia was drafted in 1682 by William Penn; James Ogelethorpe drafted the city plan for Savannah in 1733; and Pierre L'Enfant began drafting a plan for Washington, DC in 1791. The grid was a departure from the earlier cities that were circular in form.[11] Population considerations may have accounted for this change. Family structures were altered when population started increasing. Therefore, meeting the nutritional requirements of an increasing population became difficult. Many European towns were surrounded by constricting rings of fortification. England's development, for instance, was as a result of its island location that created a form of protection and defense. England has not been invaded since 1066.[12]

Another catalyst for the change in nature of city planning was the advancement in defense structures. The invention of gun powder created problems for middle-aged colonial towns. Before that, cities could be protected by palisades or walls. Earthworks became necessary and attackers had to be met with flanking fire. The castle acquired projecting towers and ramparts were fitted with bastions.[13] Religion played an important role in the behavior and character of inhabitants within a walled city. Attempts were not made to break free because of religious potencies of the city.[14] The transformation of a castle into a village became more widespread from the ninth to the thirteenth centuries.[15] History informs us that cities were often established near rich agricultural land and water resources in order to make trade, craft production, and sustenance possible. Some older cities also developed around churches, cathedrals, and squares with tenement housing and apartment blocks lining most streets.[16] These cities did not grow beyond walking distance or hearing distance. The limits of the city were determined by how far the sound of bow bells could travel.[17]

Radial Street System

Renaissance ideas of city planning based on radial street system and centralized plans also influenced city development in Europe. Streets were laid on geometric principles to focus on important monuments, fountains, or obelisks. Streets were made wide and straight to satisfy the need for military control and the increase in the use of carriages and coaches.[18] Paris is an example of how well the radial system was implemented. Baron Haussmann's modernization project of Paris in the 1860s is a case in point. During the revolutions of 1848 in Paris, the older neighborhoods were susceptible to revolts because people frequently barricaded the narrow streets for defense purposes during times of upheaval. His role was to make Paris a capital city suitable for an imperial power and this involved modernizing for an expanding population, solving the issues of traffic, and creating an environment for industrialization.[19] The overcrowded neighborhoods of Paris with narrow streets were torn down and replaced by the bourgeois housing and wide boulevards. The new urban design displaced and dispersed many of these rebellious populations while the avenue allowed troops to easily march into neighborhoods and restore order.[20] This led to the preference for wider streets in other countries. After Napoleon assumed leadership of Paris, he immediately started planning a new Paris with straight building lines and broad thoroughfares that were not adaptable to the usual street-fighting tactics.

Napoleon's plans for the beautification of Paris was presented to the inhabitants. He made it a priority to get the common people to buy into it, though the upper class were not very keen. The state expropriated land and reached an agreement with contractors to demolish old buildings, construct new buildings and boulevards and hand them over on completion. The state then made payment for work done over a period. To receive the expropriation money, it was decided that the contractors, before taking over the work, were to lend the necessary sum of money to the government.[21] The capital was completely redesigned and built over a twenty-year period under the supervision of George-Eugene Hausmann. He was a public administrator with no training in architecture or urban planning. He executed the design of Paris in three phases; the plan involved the demolition of 19,730 historic buildings and the construction of 34,000 new buildings. He encouraged modern methods of construction such as the use of iron and glass, and he managed to ensure the erection of a homogeneous Classical Renaissance Revival urban fabric.[22] Architects, engineers, and landscape architects worked alongside skilled and unskilled workers to restore the city to health after long decades of cholera and typhus. Parks were built and made accessible to all classes of people.[23] Over 4,000 acres of parks and 100 miles of new streets were built.[24]

The Industrial Revolution

Prior to the eighteenth century, the intensity of the ecological impact of cities on nature and life supporting systems were not at disturbing proportions. The advent of industrialization and rapid urbanization in the eighteenth century began the war on nature.[25] The world was so fascinated with the new freedom of mobility that the effects on nature were ignored. The broad street came in before the invention of wheeled vehicles, probably for sacred processions and for marching soldiers. During this period, George Pullman built a model industrial town in 1869. The first planned suburban community of Riverside, Illinois was designed in 1869 by Frederick Law Olmsted and Calvert Vaux.

During the Industrial Revolution, coal and steam power rose quickly to prominence, and with them rail roads. Alternative sites became available for siting of factories and access to railway was the only condition to be met to deliver coal, raw materials, and finished goods. Most Americans lived on farms before the Industrial Revolution but the higher wages of factory jobs in urban areas attracted people from farming areas. By 1920 the census had established city populations had overtaken that in farming and rural areas. The population increase was also aided by the migration of Europeans. Overcrowding and chaos soon characterized cities. The population of New York City grew six-fold, and Chicago nine-fold between 1870 and 1920.[26] Soon it became necessary to determine the future physical arrangement and condition of the city. An appraisal of current conditions, a forecast of future requirements and deliberation on how requirements will be met financially and legally evolved into the profession of city planning.

In the period from 1900–1945 architects were unusually influential in the shaping and extension of cities. The dominant model was that of the dispersed garden city or suburb, laid out on picturesque lines with groups of houses of flats in a landscape, and clearly demarcated zones for different activities—notably civic life, housing, and industry.[27] Rapid urbanization was spurred by the multitude of European immigrants and Americans leaving their farms for cities. The urban society had come to stay during the progressive era (1890–1920). In 1903 the first garden city called Letchworth was built. It was a self-contained community encircled by an agrarian green belt, linked to larger cites through transportation connections. Radburn, New Jersey followed the garden city principles in its development. Construction began in 1928 and Clarence Stein helped design the city for the motor age. The desire to pursue garden city ideals partly contributed to a change in how cities were designed and how growth patterns were projected.

Urban Renewal

The fourth congress of the CIAM was held in 1933. The congress investigated 33 major cities and evolved principles based on Le Corbusier's notions of the distribution and ordering of the functions of the city, including rigid zoning, housing in high-rise blocks, and the wholesale destruction of the existing urban fabric. In the 1950s there were large-scale, destructive redevelopment of urban areas in America. Le Corbusier published the dogma of modernist urban planning in his *La Charte d'Athènes* in 1943, and its widespread acceptance transformed urban living.[28] Fragmented landownership and building patterns made wholesale land takings and demolition of stores and apartments to accommodate largescale development geared to automobiles the preferred option for the US government. Urban renewal on some occasions destroyed entire neighborhoods and downtowns built before the upsurge in the use of the automobile. This trend is what gave rise to the Congress of New Urbanism/New Urbanist Movement (1990). New Urbanism champions most of their ideals and principles through their urban village concepts. Urban villages are places where all basic necessities can be accessed within walking distance (shops, public square, restaurant, movies, and services).

CHAPTER 9

RECOMMENDATIONS FOR THE FUTURE OF GHANAIAN CITIES

It is an uncomfortable truth to many that birth rates will have to decline in the short term if Ghana is to make any meaningful progress in the development of its cities and the tackling of the housing crises. Ghana has a youthful population and so it has to be factored into any major decision making of the government. Family planning outreach programs must be intensified throughout the country. Plans must also be put in place to cater to an aging population in a few decades.[1] Retirement migration and second-home development needs consideration in dealing with the congestion issues in the urban centers. There are many single-family detached residential facilities that are occupied by single, retired individuals that can be converted to rental units with the necessary permits from the MMDAs. Such measures can help raise revenue to help with their health and upkeep. Education and skills development of youths is

Resilient Future Cities needed s

necessary. With the necessary skills and higher wage occupations, young adults can make preparation for housing projects in the early stages of their career. This may help them in using the right professionals to carry out housing development.

Economic Development

In June 2005, in the case of Kelo v. the City of New London decision, the Supreme Court of United States of America expanded the definition of "public purpose" to include economic development considerations, thereby giving New London permission to condemn Kelo's and others' properties and transfer them to another private party. The fragmentation of land ownership in Ghana requires that the government profoundly increases its percentage of ownership to enable long term planning to be effective. If we need more private investment in Ghana, then government ownership of land will mitigate the unnecessary litigation that has overwhelmed courts. The use of compulsory acquisition for private development will also have to be considered. Each MMDA will have to consider how economic development should be undertaken to reduce the overdependence on GOG for funding. Transportation and logistics, labor costs, energy costs, education and training facilities, and waste management affect a district's suitability to attract new residents and businesses. Cities in Ghana must start competing with each other for such investment. There must be real estate divisions set up within the MMDAs to search for underdeveloped properties and have discussion with owners for the necessary investments. A database of such properties can help in bringing investment into the district as well as improving land banking measures. Land banking is the consolidation of underutilized or vacant land for an economic development undertaking.[2]

Community Engagement

There is the need for resource and community centers which provide a wide range of research materials (media content, research findings, books, brochures) on architecture, planning, and urban design for communities all over the country. Spaces may be made available for exhibitions, round table discussions, and film screenings that will aid the public in appreciating the enormity of some of the developmental issues that plague Ghana. Creating awareness on global issues pertaining to the built environment will help foster an environment where community members and citizens can meaningfully contribute to community development. Issues affecting environmental sustainability like climate change, sea-level rise, resilience, etc., and mitigating measures like parks and tree planting exercises gain prominence through community engagement.

Parks and Tree Planting

The desire of property developers to undertake development of housing facilities without consideration of parks and protection of essential areas of vegetative cover has led a surge in urban heat islands, which is now at a point where it must be addressed by law enforcement. Domination of horizontal growth and the proliferation of single-family detached housing has also resulted in wanton destruction of vegetative cover. The government of Ghana must consider high-rise housing facilities with studio and one-bedroom apartments for the youth. As discussed, in cities such as Accra, Kumasi, and Takoradi there has been an intensity of rainwater run-off with flooding, siltation, and water pollution on the rise. There is lack of political will to ensure judicious use of land for development and conservation. Curbing these issues has become imperative, and community groups and individuals of all ages must play an active role in enhancing the quality of life in their communities.

Parks and tree planting exercises must be made paramount to mitigate the effects of climate change, sea-level rise, and deforestation. Maximizing urban tree canopies by creating parks is the key to reversing heat island proliferation. Wind resistant and flood resistant trees and vegetation will enhance the resilience of these communities. Giving incentives to community members to create mini parks, neighborhood parks, and parks to act as "cool islands," while protecting existing vegetation within communities, should be a common practice encouraged by traditional leaders and the MMDAs. The success of parks thrives on the active involvement of community members in its development, care, and maintenance. Volunteers from the built environment professions can team up with community members to design and undertake these projects. Wealthy members of the community may make long-term commitment of a minimum of one year to keep parks litter and destruction free. To acknowledge these important efforts, each park or cooling island should be furnished with a sign board presenting the names of the adopting individuals or groups. The signs should be displayed for the adopting period to encourage more community members to patronize the parks. There must be active professional outreach. Built environment professionals especially must do active work within their communities. They must educate community members through practical means.

Alternative Modes of Transport

Though automobiles continue to dominate city streets, current trends around the world have underscored the need for governments to pay attention to all modes of transportation. With rising fuel prices and urban congestion in all the major Ghanaian cities, the need for alternative forms of transport has become important. Most importantly, riding bicycles has to be encouraged. Cycling offers an efficient mode of transport, especially in crowded and traffic-congested areas in cities and in addition has numerous health benefits. A pressing intervention is required for the lack of protection given to cyclists on the street and city buses must be equipped with bike racks to enable cyclists to use buses whenever the need arises. The car-centric nature of the roads makes it difficult for vehicle users to respect cyclists. Thus, there is the need for the government of Ghana and private organizations to venture into promoting cycling as a form of transportation. There are bicycle manufactures in the country who would be willing to take up the mantle of making bicycles affordable and available. There are economic benefits for the local manufacturers as well. Bicycles, bike lanes, bike sheds, and racks should be made visible in Accra, Kumasi, and Takoradi. A plan to ensure a rapid and widespread adoption of biking as a primary means of transport should include:

—The provision of bicycle parking outside office buildings, educational facilities, mixed-use facilities, housing facilities, and shopping centers.

—The introduction of independent bike infrastructure like bridges and elevated bike lanes in communities where development has far advanced.

—Collaborating with urban designers, road engineers, architects, planners, and developers to help reduce the environmental consequences of automobile use by making biking transportation a priority in new development.

—Building a network of biking paths in communities in the major cities of Ghana to make biking safer and more inviting.
—Collaborating with local authorities to promote the use of bikes as a major means of transport.
—Educating the populace on the benefits of cycling.

Future of Ghanaian Prisons

There has to be a revolutionary mechanism to achieving humane conditions and greater welfare of the incarcerated population in Ghana. Ghanaian prisoners must serve prison time with dignity. This will mean proper medical care, skills acquisition, nutritional satisfaction, and provision of formal and informal education. The Ghana Prison Service must ensure that inmates spend the majority of their waking hours doing productive and constructive things to occupy their time and contribute to national development. Activities that will bring revenue to both the inmates and the prison service should be encouraged. There can be industrial wings built close to the prisons (food processing, printing, textile manufacturing, etc.) to make use of prison labor. These will help generate revenue needed for regular maintenance and make it possible for financial arrangements to be made for deserving inmates who offer essential services to the prison service to aid in their upkeep after serving their prison terms. Inmates with these financial incentives will then be able to contribute to the wellbeing of family members, especially children. Most importantly, the government of Ghana must also invest in halfway houses (a place where people are aided in readjusting to society following a period of imprisonment). Such an intervention will help in reducing recidivism in Ghana.

Built Environment Institutions and the Thriving City

The role of built environment professionals is key to the revival of Ghanaian cities. Detroit presents a perfect case study of how ignoring technical minds in the handling of the affairs of a city may prove costly. Detroit began as a military post and trading station of the Great Lakes. Detroit faced massive decay in the beginning of the 21st century, but the issues that led to its downfall were plain to see all along. For centuries after its founding, city planning was not extensively done. Persistent wars made planning difficult for over a century and its growth was stifled.³ In an effort to attract people to Detroit, the French government that controlled Detroit offered free land to interested people. The British, after gaining political control, also helped to grow the town.

After the fire of 1805, a plan of Detroit based on Washington, DC plan was drawn by Governor Hill. Judge Woodward was the one who suggested the adoption of a plan after the fire. The plan was only fractionally implemented because of opposition from residents. They were not in favor of the expansion of the town to accommodate high urban growth. By 1900, Detroit had grown to just over a million people (80% African American). The suburbs had surpassed Detroit in population, wealth, and commerce.⁴

However, the rapid increase in population between 1910 and 1920 resulted in the city sprawling because there were no proper demarcations as residential areas surrounded factories. This situation led to the inability of factories to expand and railroads were unable to make extensions to trackage. Values of residential properties dropped because of the smoke and noise of the factories. Manufacturing plants and businesses ultimately moved to new locations far from their old sites. Even at the height of economic boom, long range planning was not implemented. In 1951 a masterplan of Detroit was developed. Another policy document followed in 1973, which failed to outline Detroit's goals for development. As a result, developers embarked on scattered projects, so disconnected that it did not have an overall impact on the city's growth. The City Charter of 1973 resulted in the creation of three separate planning offices. The Community and Economic Development Department (CEDD) and Planning Departments were under the mayor's executive branch while the Planning Commission came under the City Council. With political appointees heading the planning units under the mayor, and the selection process of the two highest position at the mayor's discretion, there was bound to be a problem.⁵ For instance, out of the seven planning directors that served under Mayor Young (held office from 1974–1993) only one had a planning background. With professional planning experience not a requisite for appointment, the influence of urban planners waned at a period when it was most needed to arrest city decline. Mayor Young's concern was that a detailed masterplan would encourage land speculation and affect Detroit's flexibility.

The African American electorates were also skeptical about the activities of planners as a result of the Urban Renewal Program. Federal Urban Renewal funds were used to breakup low-income neighborhoods (mostly African American) located near the central business district. The support of Detroit planners for urban renewal caused further distrust from the residents.[6]

The administrative structures and skill sets needed to prevent the city's deterioration were ignored. Partnership between local government and private developers drove development in the city. This ad-hoc development without the guidance of a masterplan was bound to face difficulties at some point. It was not until 1992 that a 300-page document outlining planning and development guidelines to be undertaken in the Central Business District and ten planning sectors was adopted. When planning finally started getting attention, the problems had become overly complex.[7] Racial divisions had been perpetuated by the federal government through public housing programs. White suburbanization was financed by the federal government through discriminatory housing subsidies.[8] Getting to the close of the 20th century, 60,000 lots lay empty and more than 10,000 houses were uninhabited. White flight, increase in ghettos, and deindustrialization broke the city's back. By 2012 Detroit was home to 700,000 people. In July 2013, the city filed for bankruptcy, indebted to the tune of $20 billion.[9]

Role of Young Planners

Young planners have a heavy load to carry to help make Ghanaian cities vibrant. The consequences of climate change, especially sea-level rise, tropical storms, and diseases, have been outlined in the previous chapters. Climate change and urbanization have necessitated the urgency for future cities to be built with climate resilience and sustainability in mind. Planning remains a key solution and young planners must take up the mandate of revolutionizing the planning profession to deal with the global issues associated with climate change. There are some measures that have to be taken immediately to lay the path for climate-resilient cities.

To begin, there must be enhanced collaboration between young planners and policy makers and implementation institutions as well as active participation by young planners in the political system of Ghana. Presenting proposals and pitching ideas to political heads has been the norm, but taking up leadership roles in political parties, lending the planner's voice in political debates on the environment and urbanization must become the new norm. Many planners throughout their planning careers have tried to avoid participating in party politics and political debates. This has led to inadequate participation of planners in the running of cities. Many of the policy decisions are made by political elites who usually have no background in planning and no passion for city development, but who hold these positions because of their political affiliations. For instance, in Ghana, Metropolitan, Municipal, and District Assemblies (MMDAs) are headed by individuals who are appointed by the president, irrespective of their career backgrounds. These individuals wield so much power that even when the decisions they have taken become detrimental to city development, no interventions are made until there is a change in government through a general election. The political climate in Ghana requires a lot more effort from young planners to get into key positions that allow for effective policy formulation. Young Ghanaian planners must adopt new measures to enable them to get involved in decision making at the highest level of political power. This will mean more active participation in governance, more deliberation, and, most importantly, an active presence in the political party system in Ghana. An increase in the representation of planners in the parliament of Ghana must be a goal for the Ghana Institute of Planners.

Another important intervention for young planners is bringing awareness to the need for sustainable development, making their voices heard, and promoting the profession of planning. It is the desire of most planners to publish in academic journals where colleagues benefit from innovative ideas but the people who must really benefit from these innovations are the ordinary citizens who read newspapers and online news outlets to get their information. The ordinary members of society who do not belong to the built environment professions need to understand what planning is about and its importance in the climate-change era. More young planners can offer broad and in-depth opinions on issues relating to city development in local newspapers and other media outlets. This would help broaden the debate, and in the process, many ordinary people would be educated adequately. Through publications by young planners, awareness will be created and stakeholder involvement in city development will improve. Additionally, young planners must be able to take initiatives that will impact city development without the involvement of the central government. Young planners can pool resources and also solicit funds from private organizations to undertake planning and urban design interventions in cities. It is very important that planners do not leave the critical aspects of the development of our cities to the central government alone. Private participation is required if Ghana is to make any meaningful impact in the quest to build resilient cities. Young planners must find innovative ways to contribute to city development.

Finally, planning as a profession covers a broad spectrum of fields and requires that each field be adequately represented. Transportation planning, waste management, spatial planning, urban design, environmental planning, economic development, etc., remain key in building resilient and sustainable cities. The nature of development the world is experiencing now requires people who have mastered these fields. One of the most important measures to make young planners effective in building resilient cities is for them to pursue specialization in the various planning disciplines. Young planners should specialize in disciplines they are most passionate about, so that their contribution will be more meaningful. Specialization will open up more employment opportunities at the global level leading to greater impact on city development across the globe. Proactive measures and ideas are essential for the resiliency required in our cities and young planners should be at the forefront of building safe, resilient, and sustainable Ghanaian cities.

NOTES

Introduction

1. Gourou, 1966, 140. Spices were important in world trade because of their medicinal value, use in food flavoring, perfume, cosmetics, and religious rituals.
2. Ward, 1966, 21.
3. Ghana Handbook, 1961, 6.
4. Boahen, 1966, 108.
5. Gourou, 1966, 142.
6. Oliver, 1966, 121.
7. Ward, 1966, 432–36. Some of the forts and castles are in a state of disrepair while others are now museums under the Ghana Museums and Monuments Board. Http://ghanamuseums.org
8. Gourou, 1966, 146.
9. Ghana Handbook, 196, 7.
10. Oliver, 1966, 157.
11. Boahen, 1966, 129.
12. Oliver, 1966, 190.
13. Ward, 1966, 23. Moshi is an alternative spelling which is less used. The Mossis were originally from Burkina Faso and migrated to Ghana and Côte d'Ivoire.
14. Boahen, 1966, 141.
15. Ghana Hand Book, 1961, 96.
16. Boahen, 1966, 135.
17. Constitution of Ghana, 1992, 156.
18. Spirn, 1984, 9.

Chapter 1

1. Ward, 1966, 104.
2. Ibid., 57.
3. Ibid., 195. Oral tradition says the Ga people were led by fetish priests. It was a theocracy. To date the chiefs are appointed by fetish priests. The introduction of kings came when the colonial masters proposed for leaders separate from the priests.
4. Daudier, 2002, 23–24.
5. Grant and Yankson, 2003, 66.

6. Boahen, 1966, 131.
7. Gourou, 1966, 8.
8. Grant and Yankson, 2003, 67.
9. UN Habitat, 2009, 9.
10. Boahen, 1966, 144.
11. Konadu Agyeman, 2001, 17.
12. Grant and Yankson, 2003, 65.
13. Steiner and Butler, 2007, 6.
14. Grant and Yankson, 2003, 67.
15. Boahen, 1966, 149.
16. Larbi, 1996, 199.
17. Grant and Yankson, 2003, 69.
18. Report of CRC, 2011, 33–80.
19. Larbi, 1996, 199.
20. Ibid., 195. *Dzorwulu* translates into big valley and the inhabitants around knew it was a flood prone area and thus never settled there. Population growth has resulted in heavy development without precautionary measures as well as a disregard for the area's natural characteristics.
21. UN Habitat, 2011, 77.
22. Ibid., 139–40.
23. Fainstein, 2011, 143.
24. UN Habitat, 2009, 6.
25. Griffiths, 1998, 167.
26. Boahen, 1966, 148.
27. Condon, 2010, 4.
28. UN Habitat, 2009, 10.
29. Ibid., 12. The location of waste generation activities of mechanics and traders at Odawna is a permanent source of pollution of the Odaw River and Korle Lagoon. Until and unless they are relocated the pollution will continue.
30. World Bank, 2010, 38.
31. Arku, 2009, 238.
32. UN Habitat, 2009, 10.
33. Ibid., 13–14.
34. Grant and Yankson, 2003, 67–69.
35. UN Habitat 2011, 86–87, 139–40.
36. Mumford, 1961, 305, 424.
37. Owusu and Afutu-Kotey, 2010, 3–6.
38. Opoku Acheampong, 1992.

39. Buckely and Mathema, 2007, 11.
40. Mumford, 1961, 117, 108.
41. Hague et al., 2006.
42. Bussagli, 2005, 17.
43. Larbi, 1996, 196.
44. Ward, 1966, 416.
45. Mumford, 1961, 508.
46. Allen, 2002, 6, 80.
47. Yeboah and Obeng Odoom, 2010, 91.
48. Opoku Akyeampong, 1992, 26.
49. Miller, 2008, 415–20.
50. Ibid.
51. Hedman, 1984, 35.
52. Prisco, 2019.
53. Bussagli, 2005, 37.
54. Prisco, 2019.
55. Monks, 2016.
56. Prisco, 2019.
57. Langmead, 2001.
58. Lang, 2005, 152.
59. Ibid.
60. Bussagli, 2005, 356–57.
61. Curl, 2006, 206.
62. Langmead, 2001.
63. Ibid.
64. Prisco, 2019.
65. UN Habitat, 2011, 24.
66. Owusu, 1999, 238.

Chapter 2

1. UN Habitat, 2009, 20.
2. Condon, 2010, 140–44.
3. Watson et al., 2003, 7.4.
4. Ibid., 4.7.
5. Grey and Deneke, 1986.
6. Beatley, 2011, 98–99.
7. Watson et al., 2003, 4.7.
8. Larbi, 1996, 195–99.
9. Ghana Official Handbook, 2006, 549.
10. Accra and Ghana Tourist Maps, 25.

11. Ching, 2012, 255–65.
12. Condon, 2010, 10.
13. Ching, 2012, 255–65.
14. Davidson, 2004, 55.
15. Hooff et al., 2014, 143.
16. See "What is climate change?" A really simple guide. bbc.com, May 5, 2020. https://www.bbc.com/news/science-environment-24021772
17. Go to https://shipandshore.com/bbc-news-climate-change/
18. Younger et al., 2008, 518.
19. Dasgupta et al., 2007, 3.
20. Belsky et al., 2013, 6.
21. Maimaitiyiming et al., 2014, 60.
22. Kleerekoper et al., 2012, 30.
23. Beatley, 2011, 98–99.
24. Watson et al., 2003, 4.7.
25. Roaf et al., 2005, 12.
26. Grannis, 2011, 57.
27. Harrabin, 2019.
28. Beatley, 2011, 2–3.
29. Ibid., 148.
30. Grey and Deneke, 1986.
31. Steiner and Butler, 2007, 59.
32. Watson et al., 2003, 7.4.
33. Xiao et al., 2007, 250.
34. Ibid.
35. Maimaitiyiming et al., 2014, 59.
36. Watson et al., 2003, 4.7.
37. Xiao et al., 2007, 251.
38. Kleerekoper et al., 2012, 30.
39. Steiner and Butler, 2007, 57.
40. Younger et al., 2008, 522.
41. Watson et al., 2003, 4.7.
42. Steiner and Butler, 2007, 53–54.
43. Ibid., 57.
44. Grey and Deneke, 1986.
45. Steiner and Butler, 2007, 57–59.
46. Watson et al., 2003, 7.4.
47. Steiner and Butler, 2007, 59.
48. Brown et al., 2015, 119.

49. Kleerekoper et al., 2012, 31.
50. Presentation by Cristina Contreras Casado at the Global Conference on Sustainable and Resilient Infrastructure in Madrid, Spain. October 30, 2017.
51. Allen, 2002.
52. Ibid.
53. Condon, 2010, 73.
54. Lo, 2018.
55. Chronopolous, 2014, 208–13.
56. Beatley, 2009, 26.
57. Nogrady, 2016.
58. Beatley, 2009, 86.
59. Langmead, 2001.
60. Nogrady, 2016.

Chapter 3

1. Watson et al., 2003, 7.4.
2. Ibid., 4.7.
3. Steiner and Butler, 2007, 59.
4. Beatley, 2011, 4.
5. Grey and Deneke, 1,978.
6. Ghana Official Hand Book, 2006, 87.
7. Ibid., 88.
8. Ibid.
9. Beatley, 1994, 32.
10. Ward, 1966, 29.
11. Ghana Official Handbook, 1961, 96.
12. Spirn, 1984, 9–13. In addition to mining, stormwater pollution from paved surfaces such as roads and parking lots increases the turbidity of rivers and streams which can harm habitat areas for fish and other aquatic life.
13. Miller, 2008, 170.
14. Rattray, 1927.
15. Miller, 2008, 177.

Chapter 4

1. Bhugra and Minas, 2007.
2. Perry, 2020.
3. Bhugra and Minas, 2007, 1,111.

4. Younger et al., 2008.
5. Allen, 2002, 80.
6. P. Watson, 2003, 5.8.
7. Holland, 2020, cnn.com.
8. Keddey, 2017, "Revolutionizing Biking."
9. Savage and Derrier, 2019.

Chapter 5

1. Moughtin, 2005, 6.
2. Rasmussen, 1951.
3. Grundy, 1977, 8.
4. National Housing Policy, 2015.
5. Schwartz, 2010, 2–6.
6. Keddey, 2019, "The Fate of Ghana's Cities."
7. Rohe, 2007, 1–5.
8. Ibid., 28.
9. National Housing Policy, 2015, 2.
10. Konadu Agyeman, 2001, 28.
11. Fishman, 2004, 19.
12. National Housing Policy, 2015, 6.
13. UN Habitat, 2011, 6.
14. Konadu Agyeman, 2001, 23.
15. Ibid, 24.
16. UN Habitat, 2011, 35.
17. Ghana Hand Book, 1961, 109.
18. Arku, 2009, 290.
19. UN Habitat, 2011, 23.
20. Ibid., 25.
21. Fainstein, 2011, 118.
22. National Housing Policy, 2015, 14.
23. Ibid., 28.
24. Bratt, 2006, 2–14.
25. Pickard, 2002, 159.
26. Ghana Official Handbook, 1961, 37.
27. Jones, 2020.
28. Savage and Derrier, 2019.
29. Fainstein, 2011, 125.
30. Hirt, 2013, 295.
31. Biles, 2011, 10.
32. Defilippis and Saegert, 2012, 99.

33. Biles, 2011, 3.
34. Anderson, 1964.
35. Lacayo, 1998.
36. Biles, 2011, 17.
37. Rohe, 2007, 6–9.
38. Ibid., 248–49.
39. Jackson, 1985, 235.
40. Gallagher, 2013, 37–43.
41. Baxandall and Ewan, 2000, 174–84.
42. Wiese, 2006.
43. Baxandall and Ewan, 2000, 184.
44. Fainstein, 2011, 5.
45. Handlin, 2004, 232–33.
46. Fainstein, 2011, 12.
47. Lang, 2005, 20.
48. Ibid.
49. Persons with Disability Act, 2006, Act 715.
50. 1992 Constitution, 29.
51. Chiara et al., 2009, 855, 881.

Chapter 6

1. Watson et al., 2003, 1.1.
2. Leithead, 2017.
3. Beall, 1997, 41.
4. Biles, 2011, 1.
5. Stamp, 2019.
6. Griffiths, 1998, 197.
7. Belsky, 2013, 19.
8. Palmer, 1995, 47.
9. Mumford, 1961, 248.
10. Allen, 2002, 6.
11. Belsky, 2013, 12.
12. Kerley, 2016.
13. Beall, 1997, 42.
14. National Housing Policy, 2015.
15. Keddey, 2017, "The Slum Dilemma."
16. Owusu, 1999, 235.
17. Fainstein and Campbell, 2011 442.
18. Belsky et al., 2013, 1–6.
19. Fainstein, 2011, 449.

20. Biles, 2011, 65.
21. Downing, 198, 5.
22. Chowdhury and Amin, 2006.
23. Belsky et al., 2013, 3–6; Watson et al., 2003, 1.1.
24. Fainstein and Campbell, 2011, 444.
25. Gupta et al., 2011.
26. Keddey, 2017, "The Slum Dilemma."
27. Chowdhury and Amin, 2006.
28. Gupta et al., 2011.
29. Keddey, 2017, "The Slum Dilemma."
30. UN Habitat, 2011, 3.
31. Owusu, 1999, 237.
32. Abdul Aziz, 2012, 11–16.
33. Watson et al., 2003, 1.6.
34. Ibid., 1.3.
35. Lang, 2005, 340.
36. Hague, et al., 2006.
37. Jacobs, 1993, 356.
38. Allen, 2002.
39. Wilson, 2012, 151.
40. Griffiths, 1998, 170.
41. Miller, 2008, 123.
42. Lang, 2005, 325.
43. Miller, 2008, 123.
44. Ibid.

Chapter 7

1. Cummins, 2002, 24.
2. Owusu and Afutu-Kotey, 2010, 6.
3. Ghana Official Hand Book, 1961, 43.
4. Grannis, 2011, 16.
5. Krueckeberg, 1994.
6. Hirt, 2013, 294.
7. Study Guide for the History Section of AICP Examination, 2007, prepared by students of Professor Daphne Spain, University of Virginia.
8. Steiner and Butler, 2007, 364–67.
9. Cummins, 2002, 107.
10. Zoning Guidelines, 2011, 9–35.
11. UN Habitat, 2011, 70.

12. Ward, 1966, 353.
13. Ibid., 354.
14. Beatley, 1994, 102.
15. Ibid., 116.
16. Clarke and Greer, 2008, 383.
17. UN Habitat, 2011, 103.
18. Clarke and Greer, 2008, 332.
19. Lynch, 1960, 83.
20. Watson et al., 2003, 4.3.
21. Lynch, 1960, 119.
22. Grannis, 2011, 29.
23. Ibid., 57.

Chapter 8

1. Mumford, 1961, 58.
2. Bussagli, 2005, 16.
3. Rasmussen, 1951, 8.
4. Mumford, 1961, 87.
5. Brown et al., 2009, 30.
6. Curl, 2006, 800.
7. Trachtenberg, 1986, 147.
8. Shane, 2011, 6.
9. Cruickshank, 1996, 1,483.
10. Brown et al., 2009, 38.
11. Mumford, 1961, 27.
12. Rasmussen, 1951, 103.
13. Ibid., 22.
14. Mumford, 1961, 49.
15. Bussagli, 2005, 17.
16. Allen, 2002.
17. Mumford, 1961, 63.
18. Cruickshank, 1996, 812.
19. Curl, 2006, 351.
20. Chronopolous, 2014, 213.
21. Rasmussen, 1951, 162.
22. Curl, 2006, 351.
23. Glancey, 2016.
24. Curl, 2006, 351.
25. Allen, 2002, 57.
26. Brown et al., 2009, 42.

27. Cruickshank, 1996, 1321.
28. Curl, 2006, 799, 803.

Chapter 9

1. Blakely and Leigh, 2010, 3.
2. Ibid., 238.
3. Go to https://detroithistorical.org/learn/encyclopedia-of-detroit/founding-detroit
4. Solnit, 2007.
5. Ibid.
6. Sugrue, 2014.
7. Ibid.
8. Solnit, 2007.
9. Davey and Walsh, 2013.

BIBLIOGRAPHY

Abdul Aziz, Abdul Baasit. "What to do about Slums?" Joint Center for Housing Studies, Harvard University. (June 2012)

Allen, Adriana, Nicholas You and Sonjo Meijer. *Sustainable Urbanization: Bridging the Green and Brown Agenda's.* London: DPU, UCL, 2002

Anderson, Martin. *The Federal Bulldozer: A critical analysis of urban renewal 1949–1962.* Cambridge: MIT Press,1964.

Arku, Godwin. "Housing and Development Strategies in Ghana 1945–2000." *International Development Planning Review*, 28(3), 2006.

Arku, Godwin. "The economies of housing programs in Ghana, 1929–66," Routledge Taylor & Francis Group, *Planning Perspectives* Vol. 24, No.3, (July 2009): 281–300.

Baxandall, Rosalyn, and Elizabeth Ewen. *Picture Windows: How the Suburbs Happened.* New York: Basic Books, 2000.

Beall, Jo. *A City for All: Valuing Difference and Working with Diversity.* London: Zed Books Ltd., 1997.

Beatley, Timothy. *Biophilic Cities: Integrating Nature into Urban Design and Planning.* Washington: Island Press, 2011.

Beatley, Timothy. *Ethical Land Use: Principles of Policy and Planning.* Baltimore: The Johns Hopkins University Press,1994.

Beatley, Timothy. *Planning for Coastal Resilience: Best Practices for Calamitous Times.* Washington: Island Press, 2009.

Belsky, Eris S., Nicholas DuBroff, Daniel McCue, Christina Harris, Shelagh McCartney, and Jennifer Molinsky. "Advancing Inclusive and Sustainable Urban Development: Correcting Planning Failures and Connecting Communities to Capital." Joint Center for Housing Studies, Harvard University. (November 2013)

Bhugra, Dinesh and Iraklis Harry Minas. "Mental health and global movement of people." *The Lancet* (September 04, 2007), Volume 370, Issue 9593, 1,109–11.

Biles, Rogers. *The Fate of Cities: Urban America and the Federal Government, 1945–2000*. University Press of Kansas, 2011.

Blakely, Edward J. and Nancy Green Leigh. *Planning Local Economic Development, Theory and Practice*, Fourth Edition. Los Angeles: SAGE, 2010.

Boahen, A. Adu. *Topics in West African History*. Schools Edition. London: Longman Group Limited, 1966.

Bratt, Rachel G., Michael E. Stone, and Chester Hartman, ed. *A right to Housing: Foundation for a New Social Agenda*. Philadelphia: Temple University Press, 2006.

Brown, Robert D., Jennifer Vanos, Natasha Kenny, and Sandra Lenzholzer. "Designing Urban Parks that ameliorate the effects of climate change." *Elsevier, Landscape and urban planning* 138 (2015): 118–31.

Brown, Lance Jay, David Dixon, and Oliver Gillham. *Urban Design for an Urban Century, place making for people*. New Jersey: John Wiley and Sons, 2009.

Buckley, Robert M. and Ashna S. Mathema. "Is Accra a Super City?" World Bank Policy Research Working Paper, No 4453, December 1, 2007.

Bussagli, Marco. *Understanding Architecture: Styles and structures from the pyramids to post modernism*. London: I. B. Tauris & Co. Ltd., 2005.

Ching, Francis D.K. *A Visual Dictionary of Architecture*, second edition. New Jersey: John Wiley & Sons, 2012.

Chowdhury, Furhat Jahan, and Amin Nural. "Environmental Assessment in Slum improvement programs. Some evidence from a study on infrastructure projects in two Dhaka Slums." *Environmental Impact Assessment Review* 26(6), (2006): 530–52.

Chronopoulos, Themis. "Robert Moses and the visual dimension of physical disorder: Efforts to demonstrate urban blight in the age of slum clearance." *Journal of Planning History* 13 (2014): 207.

Clarke, Sandra, and Sarah Greer. *Land Law, Directions*. Oxford: Oxford University Press, 2008.

Condon, Patrick M. *Seven Rules for Sustainable Communities: Design for the Post-Carbon World*. Washington: Island Press, 2010.

Constitution of the Republic of Ghana, 1992.

Cruickshank, Dan, ed. *Sir Banister Fletcher's History of Architecture*, twentieth edition. New Delhi: Butterworth Heinemann, 1996.

Cummins, Martin. *Designing and Building your own house*. Wiltshire: The Crowood Press, 2002.

Curl, James Stevens. *A Dictionary of Architecture and Landscape Architecture*, Second Edition. Oxford: Oxford University Press, 2006.

Dasgupta, Susmita, Benoit Laplante, Craig Meisner, David Wheeler, and Jianping Yan. "The Impact of Sea Level Rise on Developing Countries: A comparative Analysis." World Bank Policy Research Working Paper, (February 2007).

Daudier, Jean Pierre. *Ghana*, Tema: G.P.P.I, 2002.

Davey, Monica and Mary Williams Walsh. "For Detroit, a Crisis of Bad Decisions and Crossed Fingers." *The New York Times*. March 11, 2013.

Davidson, Michael and Fay Dolnick. *A Planners Dictionary*. Chicago: American Planning Association, 2004.

Defilippis, James and Susan Saegert, ed. *The Community Development Reader*, Second Edition. New York: Routledge, 2012.

Downing, Andrew Jackson. *Victorian Cottage Residences*. New York: Dover Publications Inc., 1981.

Fainstein, Susan S. and Scott Campbell, ed. *Readings in Urban Theory*, Third Edition. Wiley-Blackwell, 2011.

Fishman, Robert. *Rethinking Public Housing*. New York: The H.W. Wilson Company, 2004.

Gallagher, Leigh. *The end of the suburbs: Where the American Dream is moving*. New York: Portfolio/Penguin, 2013.

Glancey, Jonathan. "The Man who created Paris." January 26, 2016.https://www.bbc.com/culture/article/20160126-how-a-modern-city-was-born

Gourrou, Peirre. *The Tropical World: Its Social and Economic Conditions and Its Future status*, Fourth Edition. London: Longman Group Ltd., 1966.

Government of Ghana. "Accra and Ghana Tourist Maps, Special Edition dedicated to Ghana's 50th Independence Anniversary." 2003

Government of Ghana. "Ghana, An Official Handbook," 1961 Edition.

Government of Ghana. "Ghana, An Official Handbook," 2006 Edition.

Government of Ghana. "Persons with Disability Act 2006," Act 715, Assembly Press.

Government of Ghana. "Zoning Guidelines and Planning Standards," Ministry of Environment, Science and Technology. 2011.

Government of Ghana. "National Housing Policy," Ministry of Water Resources, Works and Housing. 2015.

Government of Ghana. "Report of the Constitution Review Commission. From a political to a developmental constitution." 2011.

Grannis, Jessica. "Adaptation Tool Kit: Sea level Rise and Coastal Land-Use, how governments can use land use practices to adapt to Sea-Level Rise." Georgetown Climate Center. (October 2011)

Grant, R. and P. Yankson. "City Profile: Accra." *Cities* Vol. 20, No. 1 (2003): 65–74.

Grey, Gene W. and Frederick J. Deneke. *Urban Forestry*, Second Edition. New Jersey: John Wiley and Sons, 1978.

Griffiths, Robert J. *Developing World 98/99*, Annual Editions, Eight Edition. New York: Dushkin/McGraw Hill, 1998.

Grundy, J.T. *Construction Technology*. Arnold, London: Arnold, 1977.

Gupta, P., P. Bobhate, and S. Shrivastava. "Determinants of Self Medication Practices in Urban Slum Community." *Asian Journal of Pharmaceutical and Clinical Research 4* (2011): 54–57.

Hague, Cliff, Patrick Wakely, Julie Crespin, and Chris Jasko. *Making Planning Work: A guide to approaches and Skills*. ITP, 2006.

Handlin, David P. *American Architecture*, Second Edition. London: Thames and Hudson Limited, 2004.

Harrabin, Roger. "Climate Change: England Flood Planners "Must prepare for worst." May 9, 2019. https://www.bbc.com/news/science-environment-48206325?ns_campaign=bbcnews&

Hedman, Richard and Andrew Jaszewski. *Fundamentals of Urban Design*. Chicago: Planning Press American Planning Association, 1984.

Hirt, Sonia. "Home, Sweet Home: American Residential Zoning in Comparative Perspective." *Journal of Planning Education and Research*, Sage. 2013

Holland, Oscar. "Our Cities may never look the same again after the pandemic." May 10, 2020. https://edition.cnn.com/style/article/cities-design-coronavirus/index.html

Hooff, T. Van, B. Blocken, J.L.M. Hensen, and H.J.P. Timmermans. "On the predicted effectiveness of climate adaptation measures for residential buildings." Elsevier, *Building and Environment* 83(2015): 142–58.

Jackson, Kenneth T. *Crabgrass Frontier: The Suburbanization of the United States*. Oxford: Oxford University Press, 1985.

Jacobs, Jane. *The Death and Life of Great American Cities*, Modern Library Edition. New York: Modern Library, 2011.

Jones, Jessica. "Why flats dominate Spain's housing market." May 11, 2020. https://www.bbc.com/worklife/article/20200506-why-do-flats-dominate-spains-housing-market

Keddey, K. "Revolutionizing Biking in Ghana." *The Ghanaian Times*, March 6, 2017.

Keddey, K. "The Fate of Ghana's Cities: Redefining the Architect's Role." *Daily Graphic*, September 16. 2019.

Keddey, K. "The Slum Dilemma." *Business and Financial Times*, February 15, 2017.

Kerley, Paul. "Great Fire: The Grid System for London that never happened." February 3, 2016. https://www.bbc.com/news/magazine-35418272

Kleerekoper, Laura, Marjolein van Esch and Tadeo Baldiri Salcedo. "How to make a city climate-proof, addressing the urban heat island effect." Elsevier, Resources, *Conservation and Recycling* 64 (2012): 30–38.

Konadu-Agyeman, Kwadwo. "A survey of housing conditions and characteristics in Accra, an African city." *Habitat International* 25 (2001): 15–34.

Krueckeberg, Donald A. *The American Planner: Biographies and Recollections*, Second Edition. New York: Routledge, 1994.

Lacayo, Richard. "William Levitt-Suburban Legend." *Time Magazine*, December 7, 1998.

Lang, Jon. *Urban Design, A typology of Procedures and Products*. Architectural Press, 2005.

Langmead, Donald and Christine Garnaut. *Encyclopedia of Architectural and Engineering Feats*. ABC-CLIO, 2001.

Larbi, Wordsworth Odame. "Spatial Planning and urban fragmentation in Accra." *Third World Planning Review*, 18:2. (May 1996):193–214.

Leithead, Alastair. "The City that just can't stop growing, How can Lagos cope with its spiraling population?" August 12, 2017. https://www.bbc.co.uk/news/resources/idt-sh/lagos

Lo, Andrea. "Can India's Amaravati become the next sustainable city?" October 15, 2018. https://edition.cnn.com/style/article/amaravati-india-sustainable-city/index.html

Lynch, Kevin. *The Image of the city*. Boston: MIT Press, 1960.

Maimaitiyiming, Matthew, Abduwasit Ghulam, Tashpolat Tiyip, Filiberto Pla, Pedro Latorre-Carmona, Umut Halik, Mamat Sawut, and Mario Caetano. "Effects of green space spatial pattern on land surface temperature: Implications for sustainable urban planning and climate change adaptation." Elsevier, ISPRS *Journal of Photogrammetry and Remote Sensing* 89 (2014): 59–66.

Miller, G. Tyler and Scott Spoolman. *Environmental Science: Problems, Concepts and Solutions*, Twelfth Edition. Australia: Thomas Brooks/Cole, 2008.

Monks, Kieron. "Egypt is getting a new capital-Courtesy of China." October 10, 2016. https://edition.cnn.com/style/article/egypt-new-capital/index.html

Moughtin, Cliff and Peter Shirly. *Urban Design, Green Dimensions*, Second Edition. Elsevier/Architectural Press, 2005.

Mumford, Lewis. *The City in History, Its Origins, Its Transformation, and its Prospects.* New York: Harvest Book, 1961.

Neufert, Ernst, Peter Neufert, Bousmaha Baiche and Nicholas Walliman. *Neufert Architects' Data*, Third Edition. Oxford: Blackwell Science, 2000.

Nogrady, Bianca. "The benefits and downsides of building into the Sea." November 3, 2016. https://biancanogrady.com/2016/11/03/the-benefits-and-downsides-of-building-into-the-sea/

Oliver, Roland and J.D. Fage. *A short history of Africa.* Middlesex: Penguin Books Ltd., 1966.

Opoku-Akyeampong, Daniel Kofi, *The Acquisition Sale and Rental of property in Ghana.* Accra: Jubilee International, 1992.

Owusu, George and Robert Lawrence Afutu-Kotey. "Poor Urban Communities and Municipal Interface in Ghana: A case study of Accra and Sekondi-Takoradi Metropolis." Volume 12, Issue 1. *African Studies Quarterly.* (2010)

Owusu, Thomas Y. "The Growth of Ashaiman as a squatter settlement in the Tema District of Ghana, 1950–1990." Toronto: *The Arab World Geographer*, 1999.

Palmer, R.R. and Joel Colton. *A History of the Modern World*, Eight Edition. New York: McGraw-Hill, 1995.

Pickard, Quentin. *The Architect's Handbook.* Oxford: Blackwell Science, 2002.

Prisco, Jacopo. "The Cities designed to be Capitals." September 26, 2019. https://edition.cnn.com/style/article/constructed-capital-cities/index.html

Rasmussen, Steen Eiler, *Towns and Buildings.* Cambridge: MIT Press, 1951.

Rattray, R.S. *Religion and Art in Ashanti.* Oxford: Oxford University Press, 1959.

Roaf, Sue, David Crichton, and Fergus Nicol. *Adapting Buildings and Cities for Climate Change: A 21st century Survival Guide.* Architectural Press+ Elsevier, 2005.

Rohe, William M. et Harry I. Watson. *Chasing the American Dream: New Perspectives on Affordable Home ownership.* New York: Cornell university Press, 2007.

Savage, Maddey and Benoit Derrier. "The New Island solving a Nordic Housing Crisis." September 19, 2019. https://www.bbc.com/worklife/gallery/20190918-the-new-island-solving-a-nordic-housing-crisis

Schwartz, Alex F. *Housing Policy in the United States,* Second Edition. New York: Routledge, 2010.

Shane, David Grahame. *Urban Design Since 1945- a Global Perspective.* New Jersey: John Wiley and Sons, 2011.

Solnit, Rebecca. "Detroit Arcadia: Exploring the post-American landscape." Harper Magazine, July 2007.

Spirn, Anne Whiston. *The Granite Garden: Urban Nature and Human Design.* New York: Basic Books Inc., 1984.

Stamp, Elizabeth. "Billionaire Bunkers: How the 1% are preparing for apocalypse" August 7, 2019. https://edition.cnn.com/style/article/doomsday-luxury-bunkers/index.html

Steiner Frederick R. and Kent Butler, ed. *Planning and Urban Design Standards,* Student Edition. New Jersey: Wiley Graphics Standards, American Planning Association, 2007.

Sugrue, Thomas J. *The origin of urban crisis: Race and Inequality in Post war Detroit.* New Jersey: Princeton University Press, 2014.

Trachtenberg, Marvin and Isabelle Hyman. *Architecture: From prehistory to Post-Modernism.* Netherlands: Harry N. Abrams, B.V., 1986.

UN Habitat. "Ghana Housing Profile." 2011.

UN Habitat. "Ghana: Accra Urban Profile." 2009.

Ward, W.E.F. *A History of Ghana,* Third Edition. London: George Allen and Unwin Limited, 1966.

Watson, Donald, Alan Plattus, and Robert Shibley, ed. *Time-Savers Standards for Urban Design.* New York: McGraw Hill, 2003.

Wiese, Andrew. "The house I live in: race, class, and African American suburban dreams in the postwar United States" in

Kevin Kruse & Thomas Sugrue (Eds) The New Suburban History. Chicago: University of Chicago Press, 2006.

Wilson, Julius William. *The Truly Disadvantaged: The Inner City, the Underclass, and Public Policy*, second Edition. Chicago: The University of Chicago Press, 2012.

World Bank/IBRD. "City of Accra, Ghana: Consultative Citizens' Report Card." Report No. 55117-GH 2010.

Xiao, Rong-bo, Zhi-yun Ouyang, Hua Zheng, Wei-feng Li, Erich W. Schienke, and Wang Xiao-ke. "Spatial pattern of impervious surfaces and their impacts on land surface temperature in Beijing, China." *Journal of Environmental Sciences* 19(2007): 250–56.

Yeboah, Eric and Franklin Obeng-Odoom. "We are not the only ones to blame: District Assemblies' perspective on the state of planning in Ghana." Issue 7, *Commonwealth Journal of Local Governance*. (November 2010)

Younger, Margalit, Heather R. Morrow-Almeida, Stephen M. Vindigni, and Andrew L. Dannenberg. "The Built Environment, Climate Change, and Health Opportunities for Co-Benefits." *American Journal of Preventive Medicine*, Volume 35, Number 5. (2008)

Ailing Cities is a book written largely to educate and facilitate a dialogue with people of all backgrounds on environmental sustainability, architecture, urban planning, and design. It has been necessitated by urban ills in Ghana and other sub–Saharan African countries. Urbanization has led to the creation of informal settlements within communities in sub-Saharan countries that are most vulnerable to the effects of climate change, coupled with the lack of enforcement of planning and building laws that have resulted in spatial chaos and vegetative depletion. *Ailing Cities* addresses relevant topics essential to give the reader an understanding of how individuals and communities can bring lasting changes to their communities.